Gambling
on Authenticity

AMERICAN INDIAN STUDIES SERIES

Bawaajimo: A Dialect of Dreams in Anishinaabe Language and Literature, Margaret Noodin | 978-1-61186-105-1

Centering Anishinaabeg Studies: Understanding the World through Stories, edited by Jill Doerfler, Niigaanwewidam James Sinclair, and Heidi Kiiwetinepinesiik Stark | 978-1-61186-067-2

Curator of Ephemera at the New Museum for Archaic Media, Heid E. Erdrich | 978-1-61186-246-1

Document of Expectations, Devon Abbott Mihesuah | 978-1-61186-011-5

Dragonfly Dance, Denise K. Lajimodiere | 978-0-87013-982-6

Facing the Future: The Indian Child Welfare Act at 30, edited by Matthew L. M. Fletcher, Wenona T. Singel, and Kathryn E. Fort | 978-0-87013-860-7

Follow the Blackbirds, Gwen Nell Westerman | 978-1-61186-092-4

Gambling on Authenticity: Gaming, the Noble Savage, and the Not-So-New Indian, edited by Becca Gercken and Julie Pelletier | 978-1-61186-256-0

Indian Country: Telling a Story in a Digital Age, Victoria L. LaPoe and Benjamin Rex LaPoe II | 978-1-61186-226-3

The Indian Who Bombed Berlin and Other Stories, Ralph Salisbury | 978-0-87013-847-8

Masculindians: Conversations about Indigenous Manhood, edited by Sam McKegney| 978-1-61186-129-7

Mediating Indianness, edited by Cathy Covell Waegner | 978-1-61186-151-8

The Murder of Joe White: Ojibwe Leadership and Colonialism in Wisconsin, Erik M. Redix | 978-1-61186-145-7

National Monuments, Heid E. Erdrich | 978-0-87013-848-5

Ogimawkwe Mitigwaki (Queen of the Woods), Simon Pokagon | 978-0-87013-987-1

Ottawa Stories from the Springs: anishinaabe dibaadjimowinan wodi gaa binjibaamigak wodi mookodjiwong e zhinikaadek, translated and edited by Howard Webkamigad | 978-1-61186-137-2

Plain of Jars and Other Stories, Geary Hobson | 978-0-87013-998-7

Sacred Wilderness, Susan Power | 978-1-61186-111-2

Seeing Red—Hollywood's Pixeled Skins: American Indians and Film, edited by LeAnne Howe, Harvey Markowitz, and Denise K. Cummings | 978-1-61186-081-8

Shedding Skins: Four Sioux Poets, edited by Adrian C. Louis | 978-0-87013-823-2

Stories for a Lost Child, Carter Meland | 978-1-61186-244-7

Stories through Theories/Theories through Stories: North American Indian Writing, Storytelling, and Critique, edited by Gordon D. Henry Jr., Nieves Pascual Soler, and Silvia Martinez-Falquina | 978-0-87013-841-6

That Guy Wolf Dancing, Elizabeth Cook-Lynn | 978-1-61186-138-9

Those Who Belong: Identity, Family, Blood, and Citizenship among the White Earth Anishinaabeg, Jill Doerfler | 978-1-61186-169-3

Visualities: Perspectives on Contemporary American Indian Film and Art, edited by Denise K. Cummings | 978-0-87013-999-4

Writing Home: Indigenous Narratives of Resistance, Michael D. Wilson | 978-0-87013-818-8

Gambling on Authenticity

GAMING, THE NOBLE SAVAGE, AND THE NOT-SO-NEW INDIAN

EDITED BY
Becca Gercken AND Julie Pelletier

Michigan State University Press | *East Lansing*

♾ The paper used in this publication meets the minimum requirements of
ANSI/NISO Z39.48-1992 (R 1997) (Permanence of Paper).

Michigan State University Press
East Lansing, Michigan 48823-5245

Printed and bound in the United States of America.

26 25 24 23 22 21 20 19 18   1 2 3 4 5 6 7 8 9 10

LIBRARY OF CONGRESS CATALOGING-IN-PUBLICATION DATA
Names: Gercken, Becca, editor. | Pelletier, Julie, editor.
Title: Gambling on authenticity : gaming, the noble savage, and the not-so-new Indian /
edited by Becca Gercken and Julie Pelletier.
Description: East Lansing : Michigan State University Press, 2017.
| Series: American Indian Studies Series | Includes bibliographical references.
Identifiers: LCCN 2016049789| ISBN 9781611862560 (pbk. : alk. paper)
| ISBN 9781609175382 (pdf) | ISBN 9781628953077 (epub) | ISBN 9781628963076 (kindle)
Subjects: LCSH: Gambling on Indian reservations—United States.
| Indians of North America—Gambling. | Indians of North America—Ethnic identity.
| Indians of North America—Psychology. | Indians in popular culture.
| Stereotypes (Social psychology)—United States.
Classification: LCC E98.G18 G36 2017 | DDC 970.004/97—dc23
LC record available at https://lccn.loc.gov/2016049789

Book design by Charlie Sharp, Sharp Designs, East Lansing, MI
Cover design by Erin Kirk New
Cover artwork is *The Posse* ©Jim Denomie and is used courtesy of the artist. All rights reserved.

Michigan State University Press is a member of the Green Press Initiative and is committed to developing
and encouraging ecologically responsible publishing practices. For more information about the Green
Press Initiative and the use of recycled paper in book publishing, please visit www.greenpressinitiative.org.

Visit Michigan State University Press at *www.msupress.org*

To my parents, my first and best teachers.

BECCA GERCKEN

———————

To Zack and Mary Beth, who believe in me.

JULIE PELLETIER

———————

Dedicated to Susan Applegate Krouse,
Ziigwam Niibe Kwe (Spring Water Woman)
Anthropologist, Wife, Mentor, Colleague, Friend

In May 2009, Susan Applegate Krouse, PhD, was scheduled to present "Miracle on Canal Street" at one of the first meetings of the Native American and Indigenous Studies Association (NAISA), at a panel she had organized. Instead, she asked me, her former graduate student, to read her paper, as I was on the same panel. She and her husband, Ned Krouse, took a long-postponed trip to France instead. The decision was timely but bittersweet, made in the aftermath of a cancer diagnosis. Susan walked on in June 2010, her life and her work prematurely ended. The following is the abstract of "Miracle on Canal Street: Forest County Potawatomi Charitable Giving," which she submitted to NAISA:

The Forest County Potawatomi Community operates a highly successful tribal gaming enterprise and contributes substantially to a variety of charities. The charitable giving is clearly part of the tribe's effort to give back to their communities, but it is also good business and helps them maintain good relations with the public and with local and state governments. Tribal philanthropy on a large scale is new to Indian Country. This piece examines the decisions made by the tribe in their charitable giving and the image they present with their philanthropic choices. (Susan Applegate Krouse, 2009)

As sometimes happens with conference panels, the presenters were inspired with the idea of putting together a book, with our papers expanded into chapters. Darrel Manitowabi was on the NAISA panel in 2009; he and I also presented papers related to Indian casinos. As the panel organizer, Susan was one of the individuals taking the lead, and some ideas were tossed around over the next few months, between bouts of chemo and the inevitable distractions and obligations that derail the best intentions. Then, too soon, Susan was too ill to carry on. That particular book project didn't come to fruition, but we believe that she would have eagerly contributed to this book. We dedicate this book to her memory.

Contents

Foreword

NOBLE SAVAGE: She's too intense for me. And I feel nothing. No emotion. In fact, I'm off
all females—even lost my lust for attacking white chicks.

(PAUSE.)

THERAPIST: (He writes furiously on a yellow pad, but says nothing.)

NOBLE SAVAGE: People expect me to be strong. Wise. Stoic. Without guilt. A man
capable of a few symbolic acts. Ugh—is that what I'm supposed to say?

THERAPIST: (He continues writing.)

NOBLE SAVAGE: I don't feel like maiming. Scalping. Burning wagon trains. I'm
developing hemorrhoids from riding bareback. It's an impossible role. The truth
is I'm conflicted. I don't know who I am. What should I do, Doc?

THERAPIST: I'm afraid we've run out of time. Let's take this up during our next visit.

've been thinking about American Indians as "Noble Savages" for decades, hence,
the series of Noble Savage poems in *Evidence of Red* (2005). Recently one of my
new poems, "Noble Savage Learns to Tweet" from *99 Poems for the 99 Percent:
An Anthology of Poetry,* has had new life as a video poem.[1]

All this interest in "noble savagery" comes from my brother and me watching black-and-white Westerns as teenagers, although we didn't have the vocabulary to discuss them in, *uh-hem*, sophisticated ways. What follows is more or less an accurate account of our dialogue after seeing a weekly Western on Oklahoma City's Channel Five.

"Crap," I say as the end credits roll.

My brother shrugs. "Whaddaya expect; it's *Stagecoach*[2] and John Wayne."

Some might call this rhetorical style stoic. I prefer concise.

Same time the next week. Another Western. Indians shot to pieces.

"Crap."

"Whaddaya expect; it's *Arizona*[3] and Jean Arthur," says my brother.

The following week.

"Crap."

"Whaddaya expect; it's *Duel in the Sun*[4] and Gregory Peck."

(By now you know what I said.)

"Whaddaya expect; it's *Broken Arrow*[5] and Jimmy Stewart."

Silence.

"Whaddaya expect; it's *Broken Lance*[6] and Spencer Tracy."

"Crimony." (Developing verbal skills.)

"Whaddaya expect; it's *The Unforgiven*[7] and Audrey Hepburn."

"$%*@$#*@!" (Taking the Lord's name in vain.)

Then one Friday night, Channel Five had a salute to silent films, and we watch our first and last silent Western together. My brother, bored witless, says he'll never watch another silent film as long as he lives.

"Whaddaya expect," I say. "It's Douglas Fairbanks."

"Crapp*o*," says my brother, adding the "o" for emphasis. "Westerns are all the same; Indians are either suck-ups to white people, or they are the bad guys."

That about sums up our viewing experiences in the late 1960s. At the time there were two kinds of movie roles for Indians in film: Noble Savages or just plain Savages; both were played by non-Indian actors. My brother and I didn't know these terms, but were developing our movie critic's skills. Instead of thumbs up or down, the simple one-word "crap" was used.

Today American Indians and American Indian Nations have made great strides in economic development because of Indian gaming. Each summer and all holidays I return home to Ada, Oklahoma, where my grandmother and mother once lived.

Their home is now mine. Ada is the seat of the government for the Chickasaw Nation, whose lands include the south-central region of Oklahoma. Located in Ada proper are the Chickasaw Nation's Arts and Humanities complex, the Chickasaw Nation hospital, a Bedré Chocolatier gift shop, and many other tribal businesses. In the Chickasaw Nation's 2011 report to the Oklahoma Indian Affairs Commission, the Chickasaw Nation operations include seventeen casinos, eighteen smoke shops, a chocolate factory in Davis, a hospital, several museums, and a publishing house, with a combined economic impact of $13 billion annually. The tribe employs some 10,000 people and is growing by leaps every year.

Yet the image of the Noble Savage still prevails across America, its history dating back to early filmmakers. Film scholar and Washington and Lee University professor Harvey Markowitz has demonstrated in his insightful introduction in *Seeing Red—Hollywood's Pixeled Skins: American Indians and Film*[8] that early American films lacked an identity of their own until exhibitors showed an interest in Indians and Western themes. Markowitz writes:

> Given the concomitant rise in U.S. nationalism and world influence beginning in the early twentieth century, it should come as no surprise that some of these features focused on the challenges of creating movies that both reflected and promoted American identity and exceptionalism. Consider the editorial "What Is an American Subject?," which appeared in the January 22, 1910 edition of *The Moving Picture World*. The inspiration for this piece emerged from its author's discovery of two growing sentiments among U.S. motion-picture exhibitors, both in keeping with the nationalistic temper of the times: first, "the desirability of providing American film subjects for American motion picture audiences . . . as against the imported film that . . . usually has the drawback of not dealing with a subject suitable for an American audience," and second, the "urgent necessity of American subjects made by American labor."[9]

Markowitz further writes that "the beginning of the filmmaking industry in the United States suffered from an identity crisis. What would come to signal 'American' for early film exhibitors would be Indians, either as subjects or the absent presence in Westerns."[10] In this way American films are symbiotically connected with the images of Noble Savages or Savages as a baby's umbilical cord is tied to its mother. As a result, the consequences for American Indians have been detrimental to the ways in which we see ourselves.

Psychologist and University of Arizona professor Stephanie A. Fryberg has shown in her research that the effects of "Indian stereotypes" contribute to low self-esteem, lower grades in school, and high dropout rates of American Indians in high school and college.

> Contemporary American Indians, for example, exist beyond the reach of most Americans. That is, most Americans have no direct, personal experience with American Indians (Pewewardy, 1995). The relative invisibility of American Indians is, in part, the result of population size and segregated residential living. American Indians constitute 1.5% of the American population (U.S. Census Bureau, 2006), and about 34% of American Indians live on Indian reservations (U.S. Census Bureau, 2006). Moreover, only 57% of American Indians live in metropolitan areas, which is the lowest metropolitan percentage of any racial group (Office of Minority Health, 2008). One consequence of this relative invisibility is that the views of most Americans about American Indians are formed and fostered by indirectly acquired information (e.g., media representations of American Indians).[11]

Fryberg goes on to explain that the negative impact on Natives' self-esteem as a consequence of seeing, viewing, and being confronted with stereotypical representations of American Indian imagery is endemic in the United States. "American Indian mascots and other fictionalized, idealized, and noncontemporary representations may be associated with low self-esteem and in-group ratings because they do not provide guidelines or images for how to realize positive and contemporary selves."[12]

Furthermore, Fryberg's research explains why my brother and I became such "cranky social critics." Each week we watched as American Indians failed, either by deeds or by way of life. "Indians in headdresses" continue to show up in contemporary movies that are not about American Indians. Films as wide-ranging as *De-Lovely* (2004), *The Birdcage* (1996), *Blazing Saddles* (1974), *Hidalgo* (2004), and even *Ma and Pa Kettle* (1949) all contain random stereotypical images of Indians that early filmmakers solidified.

Like the Noble Savage in my poem, American Indians suffer from an identity crisis that is difficult to escape even in the twenty-first century. The essays in *Gambling on Authenticity: Gaming, the Noble Savage and the Not-So-New Indian* edited by Gercken and Pelletier seek to complicate, enlighten, and trouble the stereotypes that still haunt us, or send us to therapy. That is, if we are fortunate enough to live in a community that has a therapist.

NOTES

LeAnne Howe, *Evidence of Red* (Cambridge: Salt Publishing, 2005), 78. Excerpts of the foreword are from "Imagine There's No Cowboy, It's Easy if You Try," in *Branding the American West: Paintings and Films, 1900–1950*, ed. Marian Wardle and Sarah E. Boehme, 162–81 (Norman: University of Oklahoma Press, 2016); and the introduction to *Seeing Red—Hollywood's Pixeled Skins: American Indians and Film*, ed. LeAnne Howe, Harvey Markowitz, and Denise K. Cummings, vii–xix (East Lansing: Michigan State University Press, 2013).

1. LeAnne Howe, "Noble Savage Learns to Tweet," in *99 Poems for the 99 Percent: An Anthology of Poetry*, ed. Dean Rader (San Francisco: 99: The Press, 2014). See the video poem on YouTube.
2. *Stagecoach*, directed by John Ford (1939; Los Angeles: Warner Home Video, 1997), DVD.
3. *Arizona*, directed by Wesley Ruggles (1940; Tucson, AZ), DVD.
4. *Duel in the Sun*, directed by King Vidor (1946; Los Angeles: Anchor Bay Entertainment, 2006), DVD.
5. *Broken Arrow*, directed by Delmar Davis (1950; Los Angeles: 20th Century Fox Home Entertainment, 2007), DVD.
6. *Broken Lance*, directed by Edward Dmytryk (1954; New York City: 20th Century Fox Home Entertainment, 2005), DVD.
7. *The Unforgiven*, directed by John Huston (1960; Los Angeles: MGM Home Entertainment, 2003), DVD.
8. Howe, Markowitz, and Cummings, *Seeing Red*.
9. Ibid., vii.
10. Marian Wardle and Sarah E. Boehme, eds., *Branding the American West: Painting and Films, 1900–1950* (Norman: University of Oklahoma Press, 2016), 169.
11. Stephanie A. Fryberg, Hazel Rose Markus, Daphna Oyserman, and Joseph M. Stone, "Of Warrior Chiefs and Indian Princesses: The Psychological Consequences of American Indian Mascots," *Basic and Applied Social Psychology* 30 (2008): 208–18.
12. Ibid., 216.

Introduction

Becca Gercken

There are clear and profound differences between Indigenous gaming in the United States and Canada, and yet academics and nonacademics, American and Canadian Indians, and European Americans and European Canadians make sweeping generalizations about North American Aboriginal casinos.[1] Assumptions are made about the sameness of Indigenous gaming in North America, from its origins to its impact. With *Gambling on Authenticity*, we attempt to explain why people look for these similarities and even imagine them when they are not there. The goal of our analysis of gaming in its various functions—both cultural and economic—is twofold: to clarify how gaming is used to talk about Indian-ness in both academic and nonacademic conversations, and to explore what the rhetoric surrounding Indigenous gaming reveals about perceptions of and anxiety over Indigenous sovereignty.

In an effort to offer a more complete and nuanced picture of gaming as sign and strategy than currently exists in academia or the general public, *Gambling on Authenticity* crosses both disciplinary and geographic boundaries. There is a growing body of scholarship on gaming in North America, but virtually all of it focuses on economics or politics, stays either above or below the 49th parallel, and often focuses on a particular tribe's or band's gaming operation. This collection instead offers a transnational examination of North American gaming and considers the role Indigenous artists and scholars play in producing representations of Indigenous gambling. Each case study offers a historically and politically nuanced analysis of gaming, and, together, the studies create an interdisciplinary reading of gaming informed by both the social sciences and the humanities. *Gambling on Authenticity* works to illuminate the not-so-new Indian being formed in the public's consciousness by and through gaming, asking readers to consider how Indigenous identity is being undone, reconstructed, and reimagined in the Indian casino era.

■   ■   ■

The Congress finds that . . . Indian tribes have the exclusive rights to regulate the gaming activity on Indian lands if the gaming activity is not specifically prohibited by Federal law and is conducted within a State which does not, as a matter of criminal law and public policy, prohibit such a gaming activity.

—United States Indian Gaming Regulatory Act, October 17, 1988

Indians bet the future on bingo palace.

—Roy Bragg, "Indians Bet the Future on Bingo Palace," *Houston Chronicle*, November 6, 1998

It used to be that claims of Indigenous identity were most likely to be met with the question, "How Indian are you?" Now an Indigenous person is just as likely to be asked, "How much casino money do you get?" Indian gaming has entered the public consciousness in such a way that it is associated with all Indians, regardless of whether or not their tribe has a casino. The pervasiveness of Indian gaming in North Americans' conception of contemporary Indian identity has transformed some Indian stereotypes, while reinforcing others and creating new ones. Given how central gaming has become to conversations about Indians—our identity, our economy, our sovereignty—it is surprising to look back and see how little media attention it received, especially at the national level, when Indian gaming was made legal in the United States.

On October 17, 1988, when the Indian Gaming Regulatory Act (IGRA) passed, there were few big newspaper headlines and no magazine articles.[2] A simple search of newspapers in the months surrounding the passage of IGRA reveals a spike in articles in September and October, but the number never exceeds 100 and drops off precipitously by December 1988. In the few states in which Indian gaming was in place—Florida, Minnesota, and California—the act received some media coverage, but the story was local, tied only to nearby Indian nations and the potential impact on the state's economy.[3]

Today, Indian gaming exists in twenty-eight states, and 43 percent of the 566 federally recognized tribes have gaming operations. However, even with increased public awareness of the expansion of gaming and the economic and political power it has brought to tribes, there was still little buzz outside of Indian Country when Jon Tester, Democratic senator from Montana, led a reexamination of IGRA in 2014. Tester acknowledged that "while gaming is not a cure-all for the challenges facing Indian Country, it has provided numerous benefits to the communities who operate successful facilities. We need to make sure all tribal nations can determine the best possible future for their people, whether that's gaming or not."[4] Tester's comments reveal progress in federal-Indian relations: the phrase "tribal nations" acknowledges sovereignty (at least of federally recognized tribes). Moreover, the recognition that tribes themselves "can determine the best possible future for their people" precludes any hint of the Marshall Trilogy's paternalistic legacy.[5] Yet even with these signs of progress in federal-Indian relations, Native Americans expressed anxiety about the actions of the Senate Committee on Indian Affairs (SCIA); *Indian Country Today*'s headline for July 28, 2014, read, "Indian Gaming Reform: What Is Congress Plotting, and How Will SCIA [Senate Committee on Indian Affairs] Chair Jon Tester Respond?"[6]

■　　■　　■

> In order to be an aboriginal right an activity must be an element of a practice, custom, or traditional integral to the distinctive culture of the aboriginal group claiming the right.
>
> —*R. v. Pamajewon*, August 22, 1996

> Another Casino, Another Controversy
>
> —CBC News Canada, April 18, 2000

In Canada, the story about gaming is different both because of Indigenous Canadians' relationship to their government and because of their definition of aboriginal identity. First Nations people describe themselves as having status, which would be like an American Indian saying he or she is enrolled; similarly, they might describe themselves as a "treaty Indian." Claiming Indigenous identity in Canada can be just as contentious as claiming Indigenous identity in the United States, although blood quantum does not get invoked in aboriginal identity politics in the ways that it does in America. Another crucial difference in Canada's Indigenous gaming story is that provinces, not First Nations, own casinos. Because tribes do not own their casinos, status members do not encounter the same questions about casino money in Canada that enrolled members face in the United States. The differences in the American Indian versus Aboriginal Canadian gaming experience can be traced to the laws that made gaming possible. As mentioned earlier, IGRA asserts that gaming is possible because of federally recognized tribes' sovereign status. The finding in Canada's most crucial gaming case, *R. v. Pamajewon*, is different:

> In order to be an aboriginal right an activity must be an element of a practice, custom, or traditional integral to the distinctive culture of the aboriginal group claiming the right. The Court must first identify the exact nature of the activity claimed to be a right and must then go on to determine whether that activity could be said to be "a defining feature of the culture in question" prior to contact with the Europeans.[7]

The decision to allow gaming was tied to Canada's Indian Act and was not about the sovereign right granted to aboriginal people on their own land base; rather, it was about the right to regulate what happened on that land.[8] In spite of the court's recognition of this right, the court gave the power to regulate gaming to the provinces, not to First Nations peoples. And while there is a perception that American Indian tribes have more control over their gaming operations than do Canadian tribes and in fact do oversee the day-to-day operation of their casinos, the fact remains that American Indigenous gaming is regulated by IGRA. Therefore, the more crucial distinction between the Pamajewon ruling and IGRA is that in Canada, tribes must establish a historical cultural connection to gaming—a requirement not found in IGRA. This connection is to be determined by the court, a disturbing and contradictory erasure of aboriginal peoples' cultural sovereignty.

It is perhaps because of these differences in legal findings that Canada has not seen the growth in Indigenous gaming witnessed in the United States. However, as Kevin Libin observes in the *National Post*, "In Canada so far, 14 First Nations casinos have opened since 1996, when North Battleford's Gold Eagle and Prince Albert's Northern Lights pioneered the Canadian industry in Saskatchewan, inspired by the success of Foxwoods."[9]

Indian Gaming stopped being a local story in the United States and Canada long ago. People know—and have opinions—about gaming regardless of whether or not there is an Indian casino near them, and that knowledge comes from our understanding—and sometimes misunderstanding—of gaming's impact. It has transformed Indian Country and Indian relationships with state and provincial as well as federal governments. It has changed the conversation about many reservation and reserve economies and put sovereignty in the spotlight and often under siege.

This collection examines how Indigenous communities, leaders, and artists in the United States and Canada employ and subvert perceptions of Indigenous peoples and their cultural practices in the context of gaming. It also engages the relevance of gaming to questions central to contemporary Indian life, including identity and sovereignty. We are analyzing not just Indian casinos themselves, but what they have come to mean for Indians and non-Indians alike. By examining the performance of Indian-ness in the context of gaming—from casino art to Indian entrepreneurship to depictions of casinos in American Indian literature—each chapter considers the profound ambiguity of the stereotypical Indian-ness that pervades gaming culture and also marks the moments when Indians resist the stereotype not in spite of gaming, but because of gaming. We study not only these cultural performances and what motivates them but also how these performances are read.

■   ■   ■

The book opens with "Raised Stakes: Writing on/and the New Game of Chance" in which Becca Gercken examines literary representations of gaming, focusing on works by Jim Northrup, Louis Owens, Stephen Graham Jones, Gerald Vizenor, and Louise Erdrich. Gercken argues that gaming is shorthand recognized by both Indian and non-Indian readers alike and that it serves as a mechanism to foreground questions of identity, authenticity, and sovereignty in a compact yet complicated space. Her analysis suggests that contemporary Indigenous writers reveal a profound ambivalence toward gaming as their texts teach us about gaming's peril and its protection, its limitations, and its possibilities.

Heid E. Erdrich considers a different type of representation of Indian gaming through her interview with painter Jim Denomie, a member of the Lac Courte Oreilles Band of Ojibwe. Working through critic Dean Rader's framework of Indigenous art as "engaged resistance," Erdrich's conversation with Denomie about his painting *Casino Sunrise* reveals tensions between "casino art" and art that asks viewers to question preconceived notions of Indian history, contemporary life, and identity.

In "The Noble Savage as Entrepreneur: Indian Gaming Success," Julie Pelletier argues that while the influence of the gaming tribes in northern Michigan is substantial, their accomplishments are jarring in the face of the often unexamined stereotype of the Noble Savage. This chapter analyzes tensions found in the intersections of representations of Indian identity, Indian entrepreneurial activities, and Indigenous expressions of sovereignty in a U.S. context. Of particular interest is the effect of mandated profit-sharing of Indian casino revenues with non-Indian communities in the Upper Peninsula of Michigan. Pelletier addresses a largely unconsidered aspect of gaming: profit-sharing through philanthropy and gifts by Indigenous peoples. Pelletier's work reveals how Indigenous philanthropy is transforming representations in the communities, Indian and non-Indian alike, that benefit from casino proceeds.

Yale D. Belanger and Caroline Laurent address the ways in which casinos allow Indians to re-present themselves in political negotiations and cultural practice and performance. Belanger considers 1990s Indigenous strategies in casino development in "(Re)Imagining First Nations Casinos: A Necessary Response to Ensure Economic Development." In the 1990s, First Nations communities employed various strategies in an effort to convince provincial officials in Alberta, Saskatchewan, and Ontario that they could successfully operate casinos. These strategies were required to challenge Canadian Indian policy and national economic development ideologies that simultaneously failed to acknowledge First Nations as significant economic players and marginalized them on the national and provincial economic periphery. In response, Belanger argues, First Nations leaders reinvented how they approached and engaged provincial officials assigned the task of negotiating reserve casinos into existence, specifically by adapting a fluid public persona.

Caroline Laurent's chapter reflects on "Casinos, Culture, and Cash: How Gambling Has Affected Minnesota Tribal Nations." Laurent claims that the Indian gambling industry is viewed by many as a disruptive and acculturating way for Native nations to regain economic independence and self-sufficiency; while she acknowledges the assimilationist and negative influence casinos can have on Indian life, she examines three Minnesota reservations to demonstrate how the so-called new buffalo might be considered in a more positive light. This chapter considers not only how casino revenues are used and the extent to which tribal peoples identify with casinos but also how casinos have helped revive or transform Indigenous cultural practices.

In "'It's a Question of Fairness': Fee-to-Trust and Opposition to Haudenosaunee Land Rights and Economic Development," Meghan Y. McCune analyzes the public discourse surrounding the Cayuga and Oneida Nations' efforts to place lands into trust. In a study that focuses primarily on Cayuga and Oneida gaming, McCune argues that the discourse in response to Haudenosaunee efforts to regain their land base characterized whites as victims of Indian progress and framed Indigenous sovereignty as a threat to white economic power in the region. McCune extends her analysis to consider the public response to the Seneca Nation's economic development in western New York to highlight how the rhetoric in opposition to gaming changes when land acquisition is not part of the discussion.

In the book's final chapter, "Masking Anishinaabe *Bimaadiziwin*: Uncovering Cultural Representation at Casino Rama," Darrel Manitowabi offers a close reading of a casino as text through his examination of the "mask" of First Nations casinos. Located on the Rama-Mnjikaning First Nation in Ontario, Casino Rama is rich in images portraying Ojibwa/Anishinaabe culture, stressing the Indigenous context. The Rama-Mnjikaning community established a culture department in 2002 to promote culture and identity, with culture expressed as a nonmaterial interconnected experience described by the Anishinaabe term *bimaadiziwin*. In contrast, the casino portrays culture as static, primitive, and nature-specific. This chapter compares commercial symbols of culture with *bimaadiziwin*, suggesting that the casino images serve marketing interests that conform to non-Indigenous expectations of indigeneity.

■   ■   ■

It has been two decades since the *Pamajewon* ruling in Canada and almost three decades since the passage of IGRA in the United States, and gaming has come to play a crucial role in how Indigenous people are represented and read by both Indians and non-Indians alike. It seems timely, then, to consider what this role means and to analyze the various ways the role is interpreted and acted. Each of the chapters of *Gambling on Authenticity* offers strategies for reading American Indian and First Nations casinos that reflect the diversity and complexity of Indigenous corporate gaming. While gaming operations themselves sometimes rely on stereotypes of Indigenous peoples to appeal to potential customers, gaming has, through the public discourse surrounding it, both revealed and dismantled old perceptions of Indian identities while creating new ones. Chadwick Allen argues in *Trans-Indigenous: Methodologies for Global Native Literary Studies* that we need to find ways to include "the realities and representations that are not simply tribal, intertribal, and inter- or transnational but significantly and increasingly transindigenous" in our scholarship.[10] These chapters are in just such a conversation with each other, carrying the thread of representations across different theoretical and methodological approaches while working together to create a complex analysis of gaming that resists disciplinary and geographic boundaries.

Reading representations of North American Indigenous gaming gives us facts—gaming is a transformative force in Indian Country—but also leaves us with questions. What would it mean if people recognized casinos as a marker—rather than creator—of sovereignty? Most important, what is possible if we reconsider what gaming means?

NOTES

1. Because our authors live and work in two countries, a range of terms are used to describe North America's Indigenous people. While "Indian" is widely used in the United States, the term is problematic in Canada, which prefers to refer to First Nations peoples as Aboriginals. The terms used by contributors best fit their analysis and reflect the geographic and interdisciplinary nature of the book.

2. The decision in *California v. Cabazon Band of Mission Indians* (1987) paved the way for the Indian Gaming Regulatory Act (IGRA). While much of the research on Indigenous gaming in the United States focuses solely on IGRA (including the work by American authors in this collection), Indigenous gaming would not have been possible without the *Cabazon* decision, in which the U.S. Supreme Court overturned efforts to restrict gambling operations in California. Because gambling was not criminal in California, Public Law 280 (which, in 1953, had transferred some legal jurisdiction from federal to state governments) did not apply to reservation gaming operations. As W. Dale Mason notes, "the civil/criminal decision had been laid to rest with *Cabazon*," and "the cumulative effect of the court decisions culminating in *Cabazon* . . . finally prompted Congress to act" and create IGRA. W. Dale Mason, *Indian Gaming: Tribal Sovereignty and American Politics* (Norman: University of Oklahoma Press, 2000), 52, 53.

3. This coverage is similar to the media's attention to the *Cabazon* decision in its regional nature.

4. "Tester Examines Indian Gaming 25 Years After the Indian Gaming Regulatory Act," *United States Senate Committee on Indian Affairs*, July 23, 2014. Web.

5. The Marshal Trilogy refers to three cases that remain the foundation of federal Indian law. *Johnson's Lessee v. McIntosh* (1823) established the so-called doctrine of discovery and determined that Indians occupied rather than owned their land. *Cherokee Nation v. Georgia* (1831) defined American Indian tribes as "domestic dependent nations" and declared that the relationship of American Indians to the federal government was that of "a ward to its guardian." *Worcester v. Georgia* (1832) determined that the federal government, not state governments, had authority in dealing with American Indian nations; this case also acknowledged tribal sovereignty. Francis Paul Prucha, *Documents of United States Indian Policy*, 3rd ed. (Lincoln: University of Nebraska Press, 2001).

6. Rob Capriccioso, "Indian Gaming Reform: What Is Congress Plotting and How Will SCIA Chair Jon Tester Respond?" *Indian Country Today Media Network*, July 28, 2014. Web.

7. *R. v. Pamajewon*, 2 S.C.R. 821 (1996).

8. The Indian Act was passed in 1876, and while it has been amended numerous times, its central tenets remain unchanged since its passage. It determines Indian status, reserve policy, and the relationship between bands and the government.

9. Kevin Libin, "Natives Roll the Dice on Life After Casino," *National Post*, February 16, 2008, *Social Policy in Ontario*. Web.

10. Chadwick Allen, *Trans-Indigenous: Methodologies for Global Native Literary Studies* (Minneapolis: University of Minnesota Press, 2012), xxxiii.

Pan-tribal Nationalist Fantasy

Scott Andrews

"**C**olumbus Day 2092" is a modest appetizer to the main course of the essays offered here. It is a daydream, a little game of "what if," a pan-tribal nationalist fantasy.

I realize that pan-tribal and nationalist may seem contradictory, since a pan-tribal perspective crosses national/tribal boundaries. However, despite the varieties of American Indian cultures to be found in the United States, those communities do share many similar experiences with colonization, and they do share the desire for greater political and economic sovereignty. So the magnitude of my "what if" game required me to imagine the tribes cooperating fully—admittedly, this is another element of fantasy for the poem. Those familiar with the history of North American colonization know how well the divide-and-conquer strategy worked then. And now.

Being the product of a pan-tribal wish fulfillment, my poem required imagery from a variety of tribes and regions, so I have references to the salmon of the Northwest, the shell-makers of the Southern California coast, the ceremonial masks found in various locations, and the Ghost Dance that originated in the Great Basin.

More than imagining the full and secret cooperation of the gaming tribes in the United States, "Columbus Day 2092" imagines proving Audre Lorde wrong:

perhaps the tools of the "master" can be used to dismantle his house. What if the powerful duplicity of corporate capitalism could be turned against those who had benefited from it for so long?

History books like to attribute the North American conquest to evangelical agendas—the desire of Europeans to spread the Gospel in particular and Western civilization in general. But so much of the energy that drove the conquest from the very beginning came from capitalist interests. John Smith's tidewater adventures were conducted on behalf of the Virginia Company of London. Westward expansion was driven by many things, but among them were the monetary interests of railroad companies and vast government subsidies of land to assist them. Etc. Etc. And most recently in the United States, corporate desires have come in conflict with the sovereignty of the Native nations that would be crossed by the Keystone XL Pipeline, the Dakota Access Pipeline, and similar projects. Imagining that legacy of conquest being turned back on itself seems like a delicious irony. Or appetizer.

Columbus Day 2092

Scott Andrews

the letters flew
on Columbus Day
little messengers
landing on porches and desks
to tell the Europeans
they must leave
must imitate the salmon
and return to their homes

the Europeans had never heard
of the company on the letterhead:
Wovoka Real Estate Investment Trust
the talking heads on cable networks
were puzzled at first
they thought it was a Polish company

the trust had been hidden beneath
a coat of other names

a coat of papers and papers and papers
layers of shell companies
shells had once served the California natives
so well and had become useful again

the Europeans had been tricked
at their own game, with their own magic
—contracts, signatures, laws, money
hundreds of paper masks were pulled
back to reveal one dancer beneath

fueled by a century of bouncing balls
spinning wheels
thick chips caressed and stacked
by the blue-haired
and the sun-starved
the Wovoka Real Estate Investment Trust
had bought every piece of America
that had been for sale
secretly
patiently
and it was all for sale
eventually

the famous Indian poet and *Hollywood Squares* regular
Sherman Running Jump Shot used his own
personal wealth to buy a bar
called the Crazy Horse
and closed its doors on Columbus Day
—and then set it on fire
CNN broadcast his smiling announcement:
"The Happy Hour of American History is over, folks!
We don't care where you go, but you can't stay here!"

the Ghost Dance vision was not fully realized
not all the Europeans left

since many were not Europeans anymore
they were husbands, wives, cousins, children
of the joint owners of the trust
many others stayed as well
but they paid rent
they obeyed the rules of the new landlords

everything was different
after that
everything

Raised Stakes

Writing on/and the New Game of Chance

Becca Gercken

Both Indian and non-Indian readers of contemporary Native American literature recognize gaming as shorthand for identity politics; gaming foregrounds questions of identity (both individual and communal), authenticity, history, and sovereignty in a compact yet complicated space. The concrete reality of the Indian casino both mirrors and perpetuates the intangible vagaries of contemporary Indian life. In the wake of the American Indian civil rights movement, Indian identity politics, as reflected in literature and film, were often predicated on notions of cultural participation. These identity politics were dramatically altered by gaming, which for many tribes prompted more rigid guidelines for enrollment based on blood quantum, and this change is reflected in Native American literature, which itself compels readers to question the role gaming plays in today's Indian Country. This chapter examines how the tensions surrounding gaming play out in relation to identity, authenticity, and sovereignty through a study of representations of Indian gaming in post-1988 Native American literature. In the postgaming literary world, we repeatedly see characters standing on opposing sides of the gaming divide: Is gaming traditional? Is it preserving traditions? Is it dismantling traditions? Who should count as a "real" Indian, and when and how do per caps play into that decision?[1] I consider Jim Northrup's *The*

1

Rez Road Follies and *Anishinaabe Syndicated,* Louis Owens's *Dark River,* Stephen Graham Jones's *Ledfeather,* Gerald Vizenor's *The Heirs of Columbus,* and Louise Erdrich's *The Bingo Palace* to see what they reveal about the always contested, often shifting paradigm of Indian identity in the wake of the 1988 Indian Gaming Regulatory Act. Northrup, Owens, Jones, Vizenor, and Erdrich each reveal a profound ambivalence toward gaming. Their texts, which vary widely in their engagement with and assessment of gaming, teach us about gaming's peril and its protection, its limitations and its possibilities. Northrup offers occasional commentary on gaming, revealing his preoccupation with identity and sovereignty through his focus on the political and economic ramifications of gaming, while Owens and Jones limit their commentary to brief but pivotal scenes that provide expository commentary on identity and authenticity. Vizenor, in contrast, makes gaming—and all of its sovereign implications—the center of his novel and offers a scathing political critique of gaming that reimagines America's history through its lens. Like Vizenor, Erdrich builds her novel around gaming, which has masked itself as opportunity.

There has been some research in literary studies in representations of gaming, particularly for books like *The Heirs of Columbus* and *The Bingo Palace,* for which gaming is the central topic, but much of the critical conversation is focused on sovereignty or economics. Those scholars who do address the cultural ramifications of gaming focus on the history of games and chance in relation to the present, in particular how they are—or are not—transformed in contemporary texts. Consider, for example, Paul Pasquaretta's assertion that "in modern times, the gambling story is important both as a feature of traditional culture and myth and as a theory of present conditions and possibility."[2] While he makes the connection to contemporary concerns, Pasquaretta's focus is on traditional stories as they are represented in new fiction. Similarly, Norma Barry's analysis of Vizenor's *The Heirs of Columbus* argues that Vizenor's "combining of the wiindigoo and gambler figures in a new variation on traditional myths and rituals reflects the evolution of traditional texts and traditional ceremonies."[3] In the context of gaming as industry, Eileen M. Luna-Firebaugh and Mary Jo Tippeconnic Fox remind us that "gaming has ancient and Indigenous roots in the Americas; it is associated [with] rituals of play and storytelling that connect the peoples to their communal origins and destiny."[4] My analysis here is not meant to be an exhaustive study of gaming as it is represented in post-1988 Native American literature or of the scholarship of said literature, but rather a reading of selected texts that demonstrate that contemporary Native American literature can help us understand the effects gaming has, both positive and negative, on Indigenous communities. Whether gaming is central to a text—*The Heirs of Columbus, The Bingo Palace*—or presented fleetingly—*Dark River, Ledfeather*—or is somewhere in-between—*The Rez Road Follies, Anishinaabe Syndicated: A View from the Rez*—the increasing appearance of gaming in literature reveals that it is becoming a permanent, if troubling presence through which Indians and non-Indians alike understand and interpret contemporary Indian life.

■　　■　　■

Readers can track the progression of Jim Northrup's attitude toward gaming through *Rez Road Follies* and *Anishinaabe Syndicated*, the latter a collection of his nationally syndicated "Fond du Lac Follies" column. In "Gambling and Other Follies" from *Rez Road Follies*, Northrup, mocking both his tribe and the state of Minnesota, details his "reservations" about Indian gaming: "I had reservations about the Reservation's plan for gambling. I was reserved because I had seen so many sins committed in the name of economic development." Much of his concern stems from the fact that gaming is creating new negative stereotypes of Indian identity rather than dismantling the old: "Gambling is creating a new stereotype . . . the idea that all of us are getting rich from the casino profits." More important to Northrup is his perception of what gaming is doing to Indians' understanding of themselves: "Gambling begets greed. The gambling tiger is making us forget who we are as people." He goes on to write that gambling works against the principle that has allowed Indians to survive, the belief that "the community is more important than the individual." He repeatedly refers to gaming as a tiger, working to undercut the belief that gambling is the "'new Buffalo' for the Indian people." He details similar concerns in a more comical vein: "*How can you tell they liked to play bingo?* Their dog was named Dauber, their kids were called Early Bird, Postage Stamp, Four Corners, and Blackout."[5]

In "Full-Blooded White People," written in 1995 and included in *Anishinaabe Syndicated*, Northrup acknowledges that Fond du Lac Indians are finally financially benefiting from their gaming operation: "Hell just froze over because Fonjalackers got a per capita gambling payment. After almost fifteen years of high-stakes bingo and gambling casinos, we got a check for $1,500 each. That comes out to a little over a hundred dollars a year."[6] His comments hint at suspicion over the small size of the payout relative to the scale of the gaming operation, and while he is pleased that the tribe has followed through on its promise, he does not like the ensuing social changes. Thus he is less subtle in his commentary on the outcome of the per caps:

What is it about this gambling? It has taken over our lives. If we're not actually gambling, we're talking about it. If we have or don't have a job at the casino, we're talking about it. We're always talking about gambling. Now the latest subject is the per capita payment. We're all talking about the $1,500 payment. Wall-to-wall Shinnobs at Wal-Mart. Everyone is just cashy now.[7]

Northrup's commentary here is telling. While one concern—that tribal members will see no economic benefit from the tribe's gaming operation—has been eliminated, more pressing concerns remain. No one (except Northrup) is questioning the size of the per-cap payment. No one is talking about treaty rights or language loss, topics to which Northrup often devotes his columns. While Northrup is surely using humor to exaggerate or at least illuminate the tribe's fixation on something he considers marginally important—the per-cap payment—his language reveals his conviction that there is danger in these payments. Not fiscal, but social. He does not like what is happening to the social fabric of his community in the per-cap era. A similar critique is found in "So Sioux Me" (1999). In the midst of his description of how the Ojibwe language class at the Cloquet Community Center is "going great" and is "filling an empty hole inside [him]," Northrup questions "where the rest of the Shinnobs are from this rez, or are they only Indians at per capita time?"[8] His frustration that many community members focus on the monetary benefits of per caps and not the programs they make possible is clear.

Northrup expands his social critique in "Blue as a White Guy's Eyes" (1998). Venting his frustration at the reservation's "Enrollee Day," held at the casino, he observes that the roll of quarters given to enrollees "quickly disappeared inside those Wiindigoo slot machines." His language here suggests that the casino is a cannibal devouring his tribe. He goes on to bemoan the focus of the celebration, wondering why his people are not instead honoring "a date important in Fond du Lac history, like the date the treaty was signed that established the reservation? Or perhaps the date the perpetual compact was signed with the state of Minnesota that allowed casino gambling?" This comment reveals Northrup's growing ambivalence toward gaming: while he wishes his people would celebrate something he perceives to be more important to the tribe, such as the reservation's founding document, his somewhat sarcastic notion that one alternative to "Enrollee Day" is to celebrate the signing of the tribe's gaming compact indicates his growing awareness of the casino's value to the community. And of course there is Northrup's glee when his wife wins a 1964 Corvette in a drawing at the Black Bear Casino. In "Brown-Bellied

Sapsucker" (2001), he notes that "the rez car license plate looks good on the silver machine."[9]

Northrup's critique of gaming, while humorous, is so pointed precisely because he understands the inherent dangers of gaming, dangers that Owens and Vizenor represent in greater detail.

■ ■ ■

Owens directs his critique at the social consequences of tribal casinos in *Dark River*, using gaming to highlight the tensions surrounding Indian identity and authenticity on the Black Mountain Apache Reservation. The tribe's casino appears at the opening of a brief but crucial expository scene whose purpose is to help readers understand the competing Indian identities at play on the rez. The novel's protagonist, a Choctaw named Jacob (Jake) Nashoba, has "been forced back by the evil of the place." He observes that "the tribe was making a bundle, doing to the white world what that world had always done to Indians," but he simultaneously acknowledges the good that has come from gaming: "the tribe was plowing the profits back into medical centers, retirement care, prenatal counseling, a few college scholarships, housing, and investments that would ensure a cash flow when the feds or the state managed to squash the too-lucrative gaming."[10] Jake's comment reflects deeply held, well-earned suspicion on the part of Indians that the government will eventually take away the Indians' right to own and operate casinos.

More important for Owens than commentary on the fiscal impact of gaming, however, is the manner in which the casino facilitates and indeed compels a specific type of performance, the performance of authentic Indian-ness, or, more specifically, what the Anglo dominant culture reads as authentic Indian-ness. While the following scene takes place in the reservation hotel rather than in the casino, it occurs after Owens has dedicated three paragraphs across three pages to describing Jake's reaction to the casino. In contrast, he writes only a few sentences about the hotel: "At the end of the valley the tribe's resort hotel, built from old-growth pine harvested on the reservation, stood like a big ski lodge against a wide, smooth-surfaced lake. [Jake] parked in front of the hotel and paused as he stepped out to watch men in belly boats fishing for the stocked trophy rainbows." Jake is there to talk to Xavier Two-Bears, tribal chair, who is preparing to meet a documentary film crew in the hotel. His "long, unnaturally black hair" is "tied in a tight ponytail," and his hand is "heavy with turquoise and silver rings." He hires only white, blond college students to work in the casino while the Apache "play . . . the white man, a subtle and satirical amusement on the reservation." While the Indians emulate white social posturing, they work to meet whites' phenotypical expectations of "real Indians," performances that are witnessed by the hotels' white employees as Two-Bears attempts through his hiring practices to invert his mother's experience at Haskell Indian School, where she was "worked nearly to death by a Swedish farmer." As Jake tells us, "Indian retribution [is] patient but inevitable."[11]

The star of this expository scene is Avrum Goldberg, the Jewish part-time anthropologist and full-time traditional Apache Indian. He arrives at the hotel wearing "a traditional breechcloth and Apache leggings and moccasins, his torso covered by a cotton shirt and vest," with his long hair "held back by a blue headband." He protests weakly that he is "not a chief" when a woman from the film crew refers to him as "Chief Gold Bird," but he does not correct her on the pronunciation of his last name. Rather than resenting Avrum's performed Indian-ness, the tribe relies on it, with Two-Bears hoping that the film producer does not notice that "they'd pawned a Jewish anthropologist off on her as a real Indian."[12]

Through the ritualized performance of this hotel meet-and-great, Owens creates both the mask and its slippage; each of the Apache, both real and—in the case of Avrum Goldberg—created, perform their Indian-ness in sight of each other, indeed, as much for each other as for outsiders, a reading reinforced when the performances continue as a tribal council meeting begins. Are the Black Mountain Apache gaining retribution, or mimicking its empty shell? As the novel plays out, it appears to be the latter.

The emphasis on performance persists as Two-Bears ends his opening comments at the council meeting by thanking Avrum for "being Indian tonight" and saying that he does not "know what we'd do without you." Owens continues to tie the casino and the hotel together with the topic of the tribal council meeting: Avrum's proposal that the Apache "give up the casino and lodge and commercial hunting and instead become a traditional tribe again, living the way everyone lived before the white men came." While Avrum's goal is to return the tribe to their "traditional ways"—talk about salvage anthropology!—Shorty Luke tries to sell his friend's plan to the tribe by focusing on the economics of the proposal: "Avrum thinks we can make a lot more money this way."[13]

For Jake, a Choctaw, this scene in the Black Mountain Apache hotel, which he understands to be tied to the casino, reminds him of his outsider status. He is excluded from the economic benefits of the casino because, as a nontribal member, he does not receive per caps. More important, he excludes himself by his unwillingness to "play Indian" in a way that Owens's novel suggests the casino demands. This unwillingness, which is best illustrated by Jake's comment that "no politics in the world were as complicated as tribal politics" and his quick exit as the tribal council members enter the hotel for their meeting, establish him as the novel's moral compass.[14]

Dark River complicates the notion of "playing Indian" with Jessie, a mid-twenties tribal member who looks up to Jake. Jessie's Vision Quest Enterprises (VQE) at first seems far removed from the casino venture, but Owens offers subtle connections between the two. Like the casino, VQE capitalizes on non-Indians' interest in tribal cultural practices as well as their lack of knowledge—historically, the Apache did not practice vision quests. Jake characterizes Jessie's clients as "New Yorkers or Europeans or New Age Los Angelinos," and Jessie observes that business is down: "Even the Germans seem to have less disposable income." Owens also explicitly links VQE to the casino through Jessie's description of his preparation for a client's vision quest: "I picked up four pounds of jerky from the Quick-Stop. That expensive stuff. I put it in a nice simulated deerskin bag I bought at the casino shop and told [the client] it was made by an ancient medicine woman specially for vision quests." The casino gift shop facilitates Jessie's faux traditional practices. The link between the casino and VQE continues when Jessie explains to Jake what he does with VQE's profits: "VQE tribal scholarship fund. Haven't you heard about it? Any kid in the tribe who can make the grades gets help. Five or ten thousand doesn't go that far in college these days. Takes a lot of dinero."[15] Jessie's profits, as with the casino, benefit tribal members, but Owens's novel forces us to question the cost. Like both the casino and the big game hunts the tribe runs, VQE offers a commodified, even bastardized version of traditional cultural practices that lead all of the novel's characters, Indian and non-Indian alike, into danger.[16] By the end of the novel, Jessie, Avrum, and Jake are dead, and Two-Bears and Sam Baca face social if not criminal sanctions for their actions; Owens suggests through his outside-insider Jake that the Black Mountain Apache casino is at the root of these consequences.

■   ■   ■

In *Ledfeather*, Stephen Graham Jones, like Louis Owens, uses isolated scenes in a tribal casino to help us understand the identity and authenticity issues that plague the Blackfeet reservation on which his protagonist, Doby Saxon, lives. While these issues play out in the life of this teenage Blackfeet boy, they are best embodied by the tribe's older members, who are failing in their role as elders. *Ledfeather* is a beautifully complex novel with different narrative voices and two storylines that begin 100 years apart, but my focus here will be on Jones's treatment of gaming and what it suggests to readers about the risks of tribal casinos.

Jones makes passing references to gaming throughout the novel. Of the Yellowtail family, Jones writes, "give them three dollars and instead of a loaf of bread, they'll rub those three bills fast between their hands and then lay them down on some nappy green table, because this time it's going to work." He also describes one young member of the tribe as "already . . . a poker chip, out there in the middle of the table between everybody." And Doby knows that to save his mother's life, he needs to get her away from "from the casino, from the house, from her cousins and sister and brothers and nieces and nephews and friends and enemies, from all of it."[17] While Malory Sainte has a long list of bad influences, her teenage son is able to recognize that the casino is the most dangerous.

Through Doby's encounters at the casino, which is located next to the tribal museum, Jones makes clear that the contemporary Blackfeet are struggling because they are removed from their own past and because their elders are not acting as such. The encounters unfold in two chapters, each with its own narrative viewpoint as Doby struggles to save what is left of his family. The novel's fourth chapter begins with a white tourist describing her interaction with the Blackfeet, and with Doby, in and outside of the tribe's casino. She finds Doby loitering outside of her RV, which has he clearly just broken into. She recognizes him from a scene she just fled in the casino: "the boy was the same one from the blackjack table."[18] The tourist's husband has been gambling next to Doby and tried to get him to quit when he was up almost $700, but Doby keeps gambling, even as he starts to lose, even after his mother appears at the table. When he goes broke, a fight ensues in which his mother jumps on the back of the pit boss to allow Doby to escape. While Malory is indeed protecting her son, she is failing as an elder: she is encouraging Doby to escape the consequences of the gambling habit he learned from her. This scene renders concrete what has thus far been an abstraction: Blackfeet identity and history are being neglected, and that neglect is best embodied in the failure of parents like Malory.

Jones links the failure of elders to both the tribe's history and the casino when Doby tries to make up for his loss at the tables by selling a piece of his tribe's past to the white tourist for $40. The woman, who expresses regret that "all these genuine Blackfeet artifacts" in the casino gift shop "had CHINA stamps on them," nonetheless buys a "little stone tipi with Southwest designs on it" along with "a pack of postcards made from old brown and white pictures. Each one had a little history entry on the back."[19] Her frustration with the lack of authenticity in the casino gift shop propels her interest in the mysterious object Doby hands her:

> It was just a bunch of crunchy animal skin tied together with rawhide. The whole thing was black with age. It hadn't been made in China.
>
> Clipped to one of the rawhide strings was half an index card. I caught it, angled it over to catch the light from the casino: moosehide (?) ceremon. Bundle, ca. 1884, reclaimed from pwnshp (Kal) 1982. Contents attributed to Dallimper, Fr (src: "Sorrel" Lf Sr.) see dis82b/Old Agency ("Caligraph 2")
>
> The stamp at the bottom of the tag read MUSEUM OF THE PLAINS INDIAN. Then I remembered: the museum next door [to the casino]. . . . We'd tried to go earlier like it said to in our packet but it had been shut down, the door dusty.[20]

This object, which readers later learn Doby has stolen from the museum, links him to his past in ways he does not understand because no elders in his community are interacting with their young people and because the museum's apparent closure means that its version of Blackfeet history is not available for those who might choose to learn on their own. The energy and funds that could be supporting the museum have been diverted to the casino.

The white tourist, in spite of her laughter at her husband's calling any male Indian he interacts with Kimosabe, seems to be aware of the weight of the tribe's history as she cannot hold Yellow Tail's gaze in the postcard image she so treasures from the casino gift shop. She thinks she wants authenticity, which is why the historical reality of the postcard so captivates her. But when confronted with an authentic, living Indian, she retreats to the colonial nostalgia of her postcards until she reads judgment for "what [she'd] done, what [she] hadn't done" in the eyes of Doby's ancestor, the "GLACIER PARK INDIAN" staring up from her postcard.[21]

Jones strengthens the connections among the loss of identity and authenticity when readers learn the story of how Doby came to be in possession of the ceremonial bundle in the casino parking lot. Doby is thrown into the museum when confronted and beaten by Dally, to whom he owes $200. As Doby struggles for consciousness in the aftermath of the beating, he realizes how unlikely his survival will be: "the elders already, the way they look through you instead of at you, you might as well be buried in the ground." It is crucial to note that Doby makes this observation about the lack of history and leadership in his community while in the museum, which is "shut down most of the time now, since the casino opened, like they can't be that close to each other."²² This comment suggests some recognition that the tribe's present—represented by the casino—cannot coexist with its past—represented by the museum. And readers have already seen the damage that the casino has brought to the Yellow Tail family. We learn through the Dalimpere narrative that the tribe's history in the reservation period is one of starvation and disease, and by linking the museum and the casino, the past and the present, Jones makes the point that the casino is a new type of starvation—cultural—and a new type of disease—gambling. While Jones's text in no way calls for a static Blackfeet culture or for a return to an Indian or Anglo notion of "authentic" Blackfeet identity, it does imply that any venture such as the casino that puts the tribe's past under dusty lock and key is too dangerous to be worthwhile.

■   ■   ■

In *The Heirs of Columbus*, Vizenor makes gaming the center of the novel and offers a scathing political critique of both America's narrative of discovery and the federal government's relationship with Indian nations. In particular he ridicules the notion that the federal government has the power to grant sovereignty to Indian peoples; ironically, he does so by having the federal government, in fact, grant sovereignty, specifically "sovereignty on an anchor" to a casino bingo barge named the *Santa María*. Thus begins the story of Stone Columbus, an Ojibwe who believes that he is a "cross-blood" descendant of Columbus, and who creates two sovereign casino nations in an effort to sustain Indian cultures and to heal the effects of the dominant culture on Indian peoples.

Vizenor plays the trickster with his version of the judicial language that affirms the sovereignty of the novel's Indians. In her decision upholding the right of the *Santa María* casino to exist, Judge Lord, who refers to Indians as "the bingo savages," rules that "the notion of tribal sovereignty is not confiscable, or earth bound; sovereignty is neither fence nor feathers. The essence of sovereignty is imaginative, an original tribal trope, communal and spiritual. . . . The *Santa María* and the other caravels are limited sovereign states at sea, the first maritime reservations." The judge's comments suggest a causal relationship: Indian nations are sovereign, and thus the government cannot grant sovereignty; it can only recognize it, and it exists before gaming. Indeed, gaming can only exist where there is sovereignty. Yet this understanding is later undercut by Almost Browne, who informs the judge that "the tribal world was created in a language game by a crossblood and a crow on a bingo barge with a sovereign anchor." Moreover, gaming is repeatedly referred to in *The Heirs of Columbus* as "sovereign bingo," language that suggests that sovereignty for the *Santa María* "reservation" has been created through bingo rather than the tribe's sovereignty making bingo possible. This reading is supported by similar turns of phrase, most notably in reference to Panda, the robot creation of the Point Assinika reservation who has been "coded to respond to bingo, the fiscal source of his computer conception."²³

Vizenor works to resolve what can otherwise be read only as a profound ambivalence toward gaming through the notion that the founders of the *Santa María* "nation" are the heirs of Columbus, a construction that simultaneously allows him to question the narrative of America as a site of discovery and blood quantum as a measure of Indian-ness. We learn from Stone Columbus and the other descendants of the famous explorer that "Columbus was Mayan" and that "the Maya brought civilization to the savages of the Old World." The question of line of descent resonates with Indian anxieties regarding blood quantum, but Vizenor compels us to reconsider our understanding of this measure of identity with another trickster turn: Vizenor's crossbloods have the "gene of survivance" because the "European" blood these Indians are descended from is, in fact, Indian blood. Stone tells Carp Radio listeners that "Columbus . . . carried our tribal genes back to the New World, back to the great river, he was an adventurer in our blood and he returned to his homeland."²⁴ Through this commentary Vizenor questions the usefulness of blood quantums, which remain otherwise removed from the novel's discussion of gaming and sovereignty until Stone Columbus uses the proceeds from Point Assinika to fund research into the so-called healing power of the Columbus signature genetic line.

Identity anxiety moves to the forefront as the tribal members not descended from Columbus read the signature as a threat: the *Ojibwe News* reports that the heirs' blood was "an estate antidote to terminal blood quantum creeds." A tribal and federal investigator of the "signature gene" treatments testifies that Point Assinika's scientists "have established the genetic signatures of most of the tribes in the country, so that anyone could, with an injection of suitable genetic material, prove beyond a doubt a genetic tribal identity. Germans, at last, could be genetic Sioux."²⁵ The biting critique of blood quantum identity is here balanced equally with the wannabe phenomenon, thus leaving the reader to wonder if Vizenor will remain as ambivalent regarding blood quantum as he appears to be in his "chicken and egg" formulation of sovereignty and gaming. Yet he resolves the ambivalence with the most clever trickster turn of the novel: the metaphoric per-cap payment for America made legally possible by the heirs of Columbus assertion of descent.

Stone Columbus, creator and founder of both the *Santa María* Casino and the Point Assinika community, writes "in the name and memories of the métis resistance" to the president, reminding him that the "rights and capitulations" granted to Columbus by King Ferdinand and Queen Isabella, as evidenced by their signatures on seven documents, "have never been abrogated by treaties, conquest, or purchase; therefore, since we are the legal heirs of the unpaid tithe on this continent, be so advised, that unless your government pays the inheritance due, we shall annex, as satisfaction of the tithe, the United States of America."[26]

With Stone's statement, Vizenor gives us the ultimate per-cap: recognition, both fiscal and sovereign, or forfeiture of the continent. The novel here functions as treaty, reimagining gaming not as a story of money or federal recognition, and reimagining bloodlines not as a means to an end. Instead, Vizenor's novel suggests, gaming and bloodlines are about deconstructing the notion of discovery and the meaning of being Indian in both America's past and present. Vizenor creates this new reading of America through the ironic opposition of the reality of gaming and gaming as it exists in his novel; gaming, like Columbus in Vizenor's narrative, is a "trickster overturned in his own stories."[27]

■   ■   ■

Louise Erdrich's 1994 novel *The Bingo Palace* follows the stories of Lyman Lamartine and Lipsha Morrissey as they compete for the love of Shawnee Ray Toose and for the right to safeguard and honor the tribe's traditions. Gaming initially seems to serve different purposes for Erdrich's two protagonists. With Lipsha, gaming is the backdrop against which stories of failed and aspirational domesticity play out. With Lyman, in what initially reads as stark contrast, gaming is the catalyst for Lyman's—and the tribe's—economic advancement. As the novel progresses, however, readers realize that there is no separation between domestic and economic happiness and that the story of Lyman and Lipsha's bingo games is the generations-old story of greed costing the tribe its most valuable source of identity: its land. Readers familiar with *Tracks* will immediately recognize the equivalency Erdrich is drawing between the financial opportunities generated by the Indian Gaming Regulatory Act and the Dawes Act of 1887; both acts served to codify Indian identity in ways that fractured communities and split families and also changed the tribe's understanding of its individual and communal identities.

The "Bingo Palace" is not a palace at all, only a ramshackle building made to seem magical by the desperation of those who gamble there. Lipsha describes it as "a factorylike Quonset hut—aqua and black—one big half-cylinder of false hope that sits of the highway between here and Hoopdance." The Christmas lights decorating the outside mask the building's disrepair and only serve to make it look "like a Disney setup, like a circus show, a spaceship, a constellation that's collapsed." Lipsha reveals what he most wants for himself in what he notices about the "Palace": the attempts made to establish domestic bliss—or a fleeting physical hint of it—by the bar's patrons. He tells us that the women "gravitate" toward the bar stools by the popcorn machine because "they know how the light makes their eyes soft and dark, how the salt and butter clings to them, gets into their clothes." The men have their own strategies, "strut[ting] like prairie grouse. . . . A few have long ponytails that flood to their waist, or thick loose hair they toss back over their shoulders."[28] It is against this backdrop that Lipsha learns of the failed domesticities in his family's history and tries to write his own story of domestic bliss with Shawnee Ray, using bingo to win her attention.

While Lipsha works the bar in the casino, the heartbreaking truths of his family line are revealed to him in increasingly mysterious ways. The "truth and disaster" of these stories begins, as they should, in the beginning with Lipsha's aunt Zelda telling him the story of his great-grandmother, Fleur Pillager, who repeatedly survived drowning. Zelda moves quickly to her own story of heartbreak, her rejection of Xavier Toose, who loved her enough to lose fingers while he waited in the bitter cold for her to say yes to his marriage proposal: her brothers "found Xavier hunched and frozen, still sitting in a curl of drifted snow. One hand was on his heart, they said, the other clutched the bottle. It was the hand on his heart that froze."[29] The hand on the bottle should have frozen as the liquid turned to ice, but instead it is Xavier's heart, made cold by Zelda's rejection, that saps the life out of his own fingers.

In an effort to ensure that Lipsha learns the appropriate lesson (which surely is that he should stay away from Shawnee Ray), Zelda continues to weave stories of strange attachments, broken hearts, and love inspiring dangerous, almost deadly behavior. She tells him of Lulu playing with a dead man in the woods, her own father burning down the Lamartines' house, and, most painfully, of Lipsha's own mother, June, trying to drown him in the slough as she tossed him into in a gunnysack weighed down with rocks. Zelda, relishing the details, reminds Lipsha that "you were in that sack for twenty minutes . . . maybe half an hour."[30] Her stories tell not only of the heartbreak of lost love, but of the heartbreak between parents and their children—*Tracks'* Fleur, rejected by her daughter, Lulu; *Love Medicine's* Zelda, the collateral damage in the affair of her father, Nector, and Lulu; and Lipsha, rejected by his mother, June. But Lipsha does not heed the warnings and continues his quest for Shawnee Ray, his intentions spurred on by what he is sure is the ghostly approval of his mother and his awareness that his strange "drowning" connects him to Fleur Pillager.

Perhaps it is Zelda's stories that bring June's spirit to the Quonset hut casino. The same night that Zelda tortures Lipsha with family stories, June appears after hours. As Lipsha walks through the empty mirrors, he glances into the mirror behind the bar:

> And see[s] June.
>
> Her face is a paler blur than the dark, her eyes are lake quartz, and she gazes with sad assurance at me out of the empty silence. She wears a pink top that glows faintly, as does the Bailey's Irish Cream filling her small glass. Her hair is black, sweeps down along her chin in two smooth feathers. There is no age to her—ancient, brand-new, slim as a girl.[31]

Lipsha, more cautious than afraid, allows his longing for his biological mother to affect the way he sees her spirit. He notes that "she looks the way she did when I was little, those times I glimpsed her walking back from her trips to town. She looks the way she should have if she stayed and kept the good ways and become old and graceful."[32] But she did not stay, and she did not keep the good ways, and the fact that she appears to him in this casino is proof of that. She is a reminder of the dangers present in a place with drink and easy money, the place that Lipsha is foolishly using to try to forge himself a love match with Shawnee Ray.

At first it appears that June only wants to confront Lipsha for using the insurance money from her death to buy the blue Firebird that she refers to as "my car." But what she really wants to talk to Lipsha about is luck: "Do you play bingo?" Lipsha tells his mother that "I never did yet. . . . Well, hardly ever," to which she responds "Now you do." She hands him "a flimsy booklet" of bingo tickets, "marked with little squares and containing numbers and letters."[33] While Lyman is unsure of her intentions, he soon decides that the bingo booklet is his key to winning the van that he is sure will win him Shawnee Ray. And he does win, game after game: money, the van. But his plan to win Shawnee backfires. Is it because Shawnee is making the same mistake Zelda made? Turning down her true love for someone she imagines will be more successful? Or is it because Lipsha's luck is brought to him by the dead? The fact that Lipsha learns Zelda's story in the same casino bar in which he "meets" his mother suggests that it is the dangerous combination of the past—and choices made there beget by greed—and the physical manifestation of the tribe's desire to be rich, the Bingo Palace. The fact that Erdrich's critique of gaming is represented through the metonym of the "Palace"—the place where gaming occurs rather than the act of gaming—foreshadows the role that land will play in the novel.

Early in the novel Lyman's story and his relationship to gaming seem different than Lipsha's. He is the picture of economic success, running not only bingo, but "cafés, gas pumps, a factory that made tomahawks, a flower shop, [and] an Indian Taco concession." But when Lyman travels to Reno for a gaming conference, the tribe's sacred pipe in tow, readers learn that he suffers from a gambling sickness that echoes the greedy sickness of old that cost the tribe so much of their land. In the Sands Casino, Lyman is nervous, rushing to his room to escape the allure of the casino, the grotesquely luxurious counterpoint to the tribe's bingo operation. He notices the "low and mirrored ceiling," the ice cream "in a thousand flavors," and a "doorway crusted in rhinestones."[34] Lyman's fear is not driven by his lack of familiarity with this scene, but rather his intense knowledge of it.

Lyman knows he is in danger in the casino and plans to exit the building to resist temptation. Instead, he is overtaken by his addiction: "Just before he went out into the street, he veered around the shining columns, past the churning machines, to the tables." Lyman is initially lucky, up $700 in the first five hours he plays blackjack. He cashes out, but by 2 a.m. he is back at the tables. He loses his $700, then exhausts his bank account. He cashes "the loan from the Bureau of Indian Affairs that had just come in to finance the tribal gaming project." The betrayal here is not subtle, and it is wrapped in reminders of the bureaucratic tape that Lyman himself wields in spite of the fact that his own tribal history is the story of land lost in bureaucratic lies. Yet it is not this fraud that most represents the depth of his sickness; it is what he does with the pipe he has spent months badgering Lipsha for. Four hours into his second gambling binge, Lyman walks into "the all night pawn shop and got a hundred dollars for [the pipe]."[35] Lyman's gambling sickness at first seems far removed from Indian gaming. He is not on Indian land, nor is he in an Indian-run gaming establishment. But he has brought the pipe and all it represents—family and continuity, treaty and loss—with him, and thus he has made the Sands Casino an Indian casino by virtue of his presence and this sacred object.

It is in the visions and dreams sequence that the reader understands that the stories of Lipsha and Lyman, which have seemed so different, are the same story of the loss of community and tradition, and that the betrayals here are not new betrayals, but the original betrayal of failed domesticity that first split their people. The two men's different conceptions of a positive future for the Anishinaabe and their different understanding of what it means to be Anishinaabe are best represented in their visions, and the reader realizes that while Lipsha will eventually learn from his vision, Lyman will not.

Lyman, like Lipsha, is seeing ghosts, but unlike his relative, he does not come to understand the messages they bring. In a chapter called "Lyman's Dream," Lyman imagines himself dropping a stream of quarters into a slot machine. Rather than seeing lemons, cherries, or gold bars, Lyman is seeing people—Shawnee, Zelda, Lipsha. But finally it is Fleur that appears:

> The face of Fleur Pillager appeared before him and the walls melted into leaves and standing poplar, then into brush, into darkness so intense his eyes strained miserably before he shut them. He was sitting face-to-face with the old lady, listening, as Lipsha had described, to the hot rasp of her bear voice.
>
> *Land is the only thing that lasts life to life. Money burns like tinder, flows off like water, and as for the government's promises, the wind is steadier.*
>
> She spoke to him, and her tone was not the quiet blessing of other elders he knew, but a hungry voice, still fierce, disdainful and impatient.
>
> *This time, don't sell out for a barrel of weevil-shot flour and a mossy pork.*[36]

Lyman muses upon waking, wondering whether Fleur was only a dream or "maybe during his sleep she had sat by him and spoken those words into his ear."[37] Dream or real, Fleur's words inspire him not to protect the land, as Lipsha is inspired to do, but rather to use trust land to further expand business—his business—on the reservation. Unlike Lipsha, who understands the importance of his people's history, Lyman seems to only understand the importance of the future, and his future does not take traditional values of land and ancestors into account. For Lyman, land is real estate; for Lipsha (and Fleur), it is identity and spirituality.

When Lipsha and Lyman go visit Xavier Toose in hopes of enlightenment, Lipsha receives a vision, but at first does not understand it. He wakes up to find a skunk sleeping on him, and he thinks the skunk is speaking to him: "*This ain't real estate.*" And then she sprays him. Because he has not understood his spirit guide (she calls him "*a slow learner like they all said*"), she reappears once he is back home.[38] He is at first angry (and wondering whether the animal is real or a spirit), but finally listens, saying, "tell me something I don't know," and the skunk gives him his vision.

> The new casino starts out promising. I see the construction, the bulldozers scraping off wild growth from the land like a skin, raising mounds of dirt and twisted roots.....
> *This ain't real estate*, the skunk says again.
> Of course, that skunk is right, for the complex is slated to develop Pillager land, partly Fleur's land and partly old allotments that the tribe holds in common, and which is fractionated through the dead and scattered holdouts who have never signed the treaties that gave away so much of what we called ours.
> Where Fleur's cabin stands, a parking lot will be rolled out of asphalt. Over Pillager grave markers, sawed by wind and softened, blackjack tables.... Out upon the lake that the lion man inhabits, where Pillagers owned and lived, where black stones still roll round to the surface, the great gaming room will face with picture windows. Twenty-four-hour bingo.[39]

Lipsha, seeming at first more like his relative Lyman, resists this image, yelling at the skunk that he "see[s] it another way," but the skunk warns him that "*luck don't stick when you sell it.*" And Lipsha admits that "inside me, I know that damn skunk is right."[40]

The reader, with Lipsha, now understands what Lyman cannot or will not: Lyman's story is not about business; it is about domesticity and the initial fracture—the break between Fleur and Eli over the loss of Pillager land told in *Tracks*. Their heartbreak—romantic and cultural—is the failed domesticity that is bound to not merely repeat, but to become permanent, if Lyman goes forward with his plans for the casino. But unfortunately, Lyman's visions, like his dreams, do little to warn him of these dangers.

Lyman has a powerful vision that brings him new understanding and peace, but it is a personal rather than a communal message that he receives. On the third day of his vision quest, "Lyman began to dance," inspired by the "long sharp yellow-green spears of grass" in the clearing. He hears a drum, continues dancing, and remembers his brother: "Everybody thought that when Lyman danced, he was dancing for Shawnee. But no, every dance, he was dancing for Henry." His brother begins to speak to him, telling him, "*When you dance, Lyman Jr., you are dancing with my ghost.*" And as the day draws to a close, he tells Lyman that he should let go of

Henry's regalia that he has so painstakingly tried to maintain: *"they look beat, man, and so do you."*[41] Henry's message reveals to the reader, but, sadly, not to his brother, that while Lyman means well, he does not understand traditions and places value on the wrong thing. He does not need Henry's regalia to honor him, yet he clings to it while he pawns the pipe that represents key moments in his tribe's history. His people need their traditions more than they need money from a casino. But he does not grasp these lessons. Lyman's vision is individual; his brother appears for him to acknowledge what Lyman has done to honor him and to help him do so in a better way. The vision could be communal; if Lyman sought the counsel of his elders he could perhaps extrapolate the message from Henry to his plans for the casino. Instead, he plans to go ahead. He values the personal above the shared history and cultural traditions of his people, and cannot see the link between his own story with Henry and other Anishinaabe stories of loss, regret, and betrayal. In contrast, Lipsha's vision is communal, and he eventually understands it as such. He knows that the economic windfall of the casino will never be enough to compensate for the land that Fleur Pillager worked so hard to regain.

The novel ends with a chapter called "Pillager Bones," a title that brings all the pieces of the story together in its play on dice and gaming and in its reference to the ancestral remains of the Pillagers. It describes Fleur's final journey, "dragging her toboggan of bones" to the island in the middle of Matchimanitou Lake.[42] The unidentified narrative voice of this chapter is communal, tying it to Lyman's vision and the dangers posed to the Anishinaabe by the gaming operation:

> We understand that from her island, when the lake is hard and deep, [Fleur] covers ground easily, skims back to watch us in our brilliant houses. We believe she follows our hands with her underwater eyes as we deal the cards on green baize, as we drown our past in love of chances, as our money collects, as we set fires and make personal wars over what to do with its weight, as we go forward into our own unsteady hopes.[43]

While this ending may initially read as cautionary, it reads as tragic for those who make the connections to the events told in *Tracks* when money and factionalism first began to split the Anishinaabe. It invokes Fleur's rape in Argus and her fight to save her children with its reference to the gaming tables. It also echoes the Kashpaws' betrayal of the Pillagers when they used their "collected money" to pay off only Kashpaw allotments, letting Pillager land fall to the lumber company. But perhaps this ending is not as tragic as it seems. Fleur has not left the people; "she doesn't tap our panes or leave her claw marks on eaves and doors. She only coughs, low, to make her presence known. You have heard the bear laugh—that is the chuffing noise we hear and it is unmistakable." She still speaks to them, calls them back to their own history and traditions. The people do not yet understand—"no matter how we strain to decipher the sound it never quite makes sense"—but perhaps if they listen to Lipsha rather than Lyman, they one day will.[44]

■   ■   ■

What the stories of Northrup, Owens, Jones, Vizenor, and Erdrich make clear is that gaming—noun or verb—is a catalyst, and that Indians do not have to participate in gaming themselves for it to impact their lives. Gaming invokes the central questions of contemporary American Indian life: Who counts as a "real" Indian? What constitutes Indian sovereignty? Who can and should benefit from gaming? Most troubling, who should not benefit, but does? Whether they are focusing on identity, authenticity, history, or tribal and federal governments, these authors demonstrate not only that everyone is asking these questions but also that the answers to these questions are varied and complicated. My analysis suggests that gaming is not the "new buffalo," nor is it the "tiger" described by Northrup; it is a new trickster, transforming Indian identity—and American Indian literature—as it takes shape.

NOTES

1. Per caps, or per-capita payments, are the casino revenues distributed to tribal members. Each tribe determines if they want to distribute revenues among their people and what the guidelines for distribution will be.
2. Paul Pasquaretta, "Sacred Chance: Gambling and the Contemporary Native American Indian Novel," *MELUS* 21, no. 2 (1996): 22.
3. Nora Barry, "Chance and Ritual: The Gambler in the Texts of Gerald Vizenor," *SAIL* 5, no. 3 (1993): 20.
4. Eileen M. Luna-Fireabugh and Mary Jo Tippeconic Fox, "The Sharing Tradition: Indian Gaming in Stories and Modern Life," *Wicazo Sa Review* 25, no. 1 (2010): 75.
5. Jim Northrup, *Rez Road Follies* (Minneapolis: University of Minnesota Press, 1997), 209, 215, 222, 224, 228.
6. Jim Northrup, *Anishinaabe Syndicated: A View from the Rez* (St. Paul: Minnesota Historical Society Press, 2011), 107.

7. Ibid.

8. Ibid., 180.

9. Ibid., 172, 220.

10. Louis Owens, *Dark River* (Norman: University of Oklahoma Press, 1999), 51, 53, 54.

11. Ibid., 54, 55, 65, 66.

12. Ibid., 61, 62, 70.

13. Ibid., 71, 72.

14. Ibid., 10.

15. Ibid., 22, 24, 25.

16. Jessie's death is complicated. While he, like Sam and Xavier, is running a questionable business and he provides clients' with false visions through an appropriated non-Apache cultural practice, his motivation, unlike Sam's and Xavier's, is to benefit his people rather than himself. Although a young adult, Jessie is acting more as an elder should than are any of the more established adults around him. His motivation explains why he is rewarded in death with being able to appear as a vision, an "animal helper" (144), for his client, Sandrine, as his synthetic wolf suit is transformed into the real thing. Similarly, Avrum dies like a true Apache warrior in his efforts to fight off the militia with a bow and arrow. Avrum's Indian "performance," like Jessie's, is made real through his death, and both men's deaths help save members of their community.

17. Stephen Graham Jones, *Ledfeather* (Tuscaloosa: University of Alabama Press, 2008), 21, 86, 123.

18. Ibid., 28.

19. Ibid., 25, 26.

20. Ibid., 31. This passage appears to be an allusion to the Sherman Alexie poems "Evolution" and "Pawn Shop" from *The Business of Fancydancing* (New York: Hanging Loose Press, 1992).

21. Jones, *Ledfeather*, 32.

22. Ibid., 87, 89.

23. Gerald Vizenor, *The Heirs of Columbus* (New York: Quality Paperback Book Club), 78, 7, 82, 154.

24. Ibid., 9, 131.

25. Ibid., 132, 162.

26. Ibid., 160.

27. Ibid., 185.

28. Louise Erdrich, *The Bingo Palace* (New York: HarperPerennial, 1994), 41, 42, 43.

29. Ibid., 43, 48.

30. Ibid., 51.
31. Ibid., 52–53.
32. Ibid., 53.
33. Ibid., 54, 55.
34. Ibid., 15, 90.
35. Ibid., 91, 93.
36. Ibid., 148.
37. Ibid., 148–49.
38. Ibid., 200, 219.
39. Ibid., 219.
40. Ibid., 220. The scene closely resembles Father Damien's conversation with Fleur about commercial interest in Pillager land: "'There's some who want to build a fishing lodge,' he said in a gentle voice. 'They're willing to trade for an allotment someplace else'" (175). Unlike Lipsha and Lyman, Nanapush does not need a vision to understand the spiritual value of Pillager land; he says that "Pillager land was not ordinary land to buy and sell. When that family came here, driven form the east, Misshepeshu had appeared because of the Old Man's connection. But the water thing was not a dog to follow at our heels" (175).
41. Ibid., 203, 204.
42. Ibid., 272.
43. Ibid., 273–74.
44. Ibid., 274.

An Interview with Jim Denomie

Heid E. Erdrich

im Denomie (Ojibwe) was born in Hayward, Wisconsin, on July 6, 1955, and currently lives in Franconia, Minnesota. Primarily a painter (oil, acrylic, and watercolor), he also creates unique works of art in ink, oil pastel drawings, printmaking, photography, and found object sculpture. In 1995, Denomie received a BFA degree from the University of Minnesota. Since then he has shown extensively in the United States and in Europe in numerous group and solo exhibitions. His work has been placed in the permanent collections of numerous museums as well as in many other public and private collections. Denomie's work has been included in local and national publications, and he is the recipient of several prestigious grants and awards.

In 2005, Denomie completed a task of painting at least one painting a day, for one year. Much of the work was showcased in the exhibition *New Skins* at the Minneapolis Institute of Arts in 2007, and he was named one of City Pages Artist of the Year for 2007. In 2008, he was awarded a Bush Artist Fellowship, in 2009 an Eiteljorg Native American Fine Art Fellowship, a 2012 McKnight Fellowship and, most recently, awards from the Joan Mitchell Foundation.

A small group of works by Denomie contains references to American Indian tribal gaming industries. Images of slot machines, blackjack tables, horse racing,

Misfortunes ©Jim Denomie. All rights reserved.

and casino structures are incorporated within the larger visual narratives that distinguish Denomie's colorful and provocative style of painting. Among these works is *Casino Sunrise*, the subject of the interview that follows these brief descriptions. Denomie's painting *The Posse*, the cover art for this essay collection, focuses on an image of a casino. Although by no means the central subject for Denomie, imagery associated with the rise of gambling in Indian Country does figure in key works from both early in his career and more recently. Denomie's visual vocabulary grows along with his subjects and has come to reveal a penchant for social and political commentary, which arises with his works that reference legal gambling and continues into *Casino Sunrise*.

One of the first of Denomie's paintings to include references to tribal gaming is *Misfortunes*, which presents a vivid seascape in surreal colors. Stylized blue female nudes on the shore seemingly jeer at and moon three ships, which represent the vessels associated with the arrival of Christopher Columbus to this hemisphere. A slot machine sits on the beach in the extreme foreground of *Misfortunes*. The

content and the title, suggestive of both fortune and mistake, might suggest an equation between gaming (the slot machine) and colonization (the ships) or at least something less than benign on the horizon.

Another painting from early in Denomie's exhibition career, *National Anthem*, is a surreal cityscape that contains figures including a man dressed in traditional Ojibwe clothes pitching a baseball from atop a "Surplus Cheese" truck to men in suits and umpire gear atop a dark limousine-like car.[1] Behind them a series of towers, some suggestive of Devil's Tower in Wyoming or Monument Valley in Arizona, some more like enormous tree stumps, rise with a slot machine on one and a blackjack table on another. On the center tower is a brightly lit sports stadium. Behind the towers, the familiar buildings of the Minneapolis and St. Paul skyline rise amid other buildings. Some of the buildings are elongated slot machines.

The Posse, an early example of Denomie's landscapes composed of towers, includes purple and red buttes, one of which is occupied by a brightly lit tipi-shaped structure with the word "Casino" across its front. Hands reach from the bottom

The Posse ©Jim Denomie. All rights reserved.

of the painting, some with open palms, some praying, some seeming to grasp or attempt to climb the butte. Figures ride past, one American Indian appearing on a winged white horse; the other looks like a cowboy on a hobbyhorse. Between the two figures is a trail of paper bills. A vehicle that looks like an armored truck with the word "Dinks" on its side is left behind by the figures.

A complex and multi-imaged scene created in what Denomie has come to call his narrative style, *Casino Sunrise* was first shown at Bockley Gallery in Minneapolis in 2009. In *Casino Sunrise* we see a landscape populated by American Indians and others, including former Minnesota governor Jesse Ventura, who is depicted mostly nude except for his G-string, one diving flipper, and a feather boa. Ventura holds a cigar chomped in his jaw while he gestures with a handful of money in one hand and a fishing rod in another. Ventura stands on a low tree stump. Around him figures are engaged in scenes both iconic—the capitol building rises at the far center background—and disruptive of iconography: mythic logger Paul Bunyan appears to sexually penetrate Babe the Blue Ox. Elsewhere images out of Minnesota history are interpreted in Denomie's signature darkly humorous or quietly memorial style: a lynching, the 35w bridge collapse, Dakota men hunting—presumably a depiction of the incident that is said to have incited the nineteenth-century Dakota War. Opposite this image, on the left side of the painting, another historic reference is to an actual case of Minneapolis police brutality: two American Indian men emerge from a police squad car trunk. The two incidents link as one of the men climbing from the car trunk clutches a chicken.[2] Many other events important to the story of both Ojibwe and Dakota in the state are depicted in this far-ranging canvas. Also referenced in *Casino Sunrise* are a paddleboat on a river—a controversial site for casinos along Minnesota borders—and horse racing, an enterprise of the Dakota community near the Twin Cities.

Arguably a key work for Denomie, *Casino Sunrise* was recently shown outside Minnesota by artist Wendy Red Star, who chose the work for an exhibit she curated in 2014. The artist owns *Casino Sunrise*.

In discussing his work for this interview, Denomie describes how *Casino Sunrise* references other of his paintings, including *Attack on Fort Snelling Bar and Grill*,

Casino Sunrise ©Jim Denomie. All rights reserved.

Attack on Fort Snelling Bar and Grill ©Jim Denomie. All rights reserved.

Hole-in-the-Day ©Jim Denomie. All rights reserved.

Show Me the Money ©Jim Denomie. All rights reserved.

in which the infamous Minnesota fort, site of the concentrated imprisonment of Dakota people, is depicted as a White Castle hamburger joint. Several of Denomie's paintings, including *Show Me the Money* and *Hole-in-the-Day* as well as *Casino Sunrise*, reference the Minnesota state seal, the official version of which shows an "Indian" on horseback riding left, or west, presumably disappearing, while a (white) man using a plow is at the center. The white farmer focuses the image on a vision of agriculture-based statehood contained in this official symbol, which is still in use today.

HE: Was *Casino Sunrise* part of a series?

JD: It's the third image in response to, and as an update of, the Minnesota state seal. *Show Me the Money* is a smaller work, and the mid-sized one is *Hole-in-the-Day* and *Casino Sunrise* is the largest.[3] These paintings are about Minnesota history all within the boundaries of the state seal. While I was working on those two, new imagery was coming to me, but it wasn't part of those paintings. I sketched [*Casino Sunrise*] in ten minutes. It all came to me: Babe the Blue Ox, Jesses Ventura . . . it kept getting larger and larger. I'm considering a fourth including Bob Dylan.

HE: Your work has evolved over your career to cover many subjects. I wonder if you have a mental map of those evolutions and if you can name them for me?

JD: I haven't defined any. I paint whatever comes and sometimes I try to maintain a genre. I listen to whatever comes to me. There was the Renegade Series and a series of erotic landscapes—then I combined those two series and the Dream Rabbit series evolved out of that combination. Next, in 2005 I decided to do a painting-a-day for a year. In that project I did 430 paintings. Approximately 300 were portraits. Before that, portraiture was never a primary subject matter, but that project started my interest, and portraiture became fun. I still do portraiture today in other paintings—it gets the creative juices flowing. Then I bring it back to the social and political. You can look at *Attack on Fort Snelling Bar and Grill* and *Casino Sunrise* and tell they are cousins.

HE: Where does *Casino Sunrise* fit in your development as a painter? Was it important?

JD: It pleased me. I was pleased with working in a larger scale and working with little vignettes—that led to *Eminent Domain,* which is seven feet by twelve feet.

HE: What was the reaction to *Casino Sunrise* the first time it was in a show?

JD: It was fantastic! People were semicircled around it pointing and laughing and just reading it. It looked like they were watching a fistfight, some spectacle.

HE: What question are you most asked about *Casino Sunrise*?

JD: People ask about the three-headed figure—that represents the gang activity in the city and on the reservations.

HE: If you were to paint *Casino Sunrise* again, what would you do differently?

JD: The fourth image will address that—it would get larger, bring in more history, more information.

HE: When was the first time your painting contained images of casinos?

JD: The Renegade Series in 1997, one painting had a blackjack dealer flying through the air, away on a winged horse, a Brinks armored car. . . . Back in '95 what I painted was the political, treaty rights, casinos, my alcoholism. . . . There was even an earlier painting, *Misfortunes*, about casinos not being a positive for any community—but it's an available economic opportunity for Native Americans. With money comes the power and greed and seduction of the money. And people think all Indians are getting rich, but no, not every Indian. It comes down to the 1 percent again.

HE: What was the reaction when you first showed works with casino images?

JD: I don't know that there was an objection to my commenting about casinos. I don't think I get a lot of comments from people. They are intrigued but [for some] it's difficult to comprehend my work without an understanding of modern art principles and a knowledge of art history and Native issues. Most Native people will understand instantly.

HE: What are you saying about Indian gaming and casinos in *Casino Sunrise*?

JD: Well, not a whole lot. In this image you can see two Native people riding toward the sunrise as opposed to riding toward that sunset. Casinos are part of what has given Indian people more—they've got money, they've got lobbyists, they've got more power. When I have this Indian on horseback mooning the [former] governor [Jesse Ventura], he's mooning the people who oppose us like [Wisconsin governor] Scott Walker and the general public who think all Indians are getting rich. *Casino Sunrise* is about Minnesota history, and Indian gaming is a part of that history now.

HE: Has the response to casino content in your work changed over time?

JD: Enough time has passed and I think things have settled down and it's status quo, not a daily topic. But in college it was fresh and a topic of conversation and misperceptions about Indian people. I haven't felt the need to comment now.

HE: What's your take on Indian casinos and visual art?

JD: Well, I think management of casinos is playing on a stereotype of imagery of how people see Native Americans. So they're feeding into that in some ways. Some of the casino art I've seen has been Romanticism, nothing daring, nothing political, the romantic Indian and spiritual Indian. Yet money-wise, now they're businessmen, too—though management is probably still mostly white people.

HE: Have you ever had a casino buy your artwork? Have you ever tried to sell it to a casino?

JD: No on both counts. I wouldn't attempt it.

NOTES

1. "Surplus Cheese" is a reference to government-provided foods, or commodities, associated with both treaty provisions and the U.S. Department of Agriculture's food surplus program for families below the poverty line.
2. The Dakota War began when Dakota Indians, having been pushed into a small patch of land that could not sustain them, were starving. The situation was compounded by the fact that their treaty annuities were not being paid, with the country distracted and impoverished by the Civil War. Four Dakota men stole chicken eggs from white settlers, some of whom they then killed.
3. While there are two famous Ojibwe leaders, Hole-in-the-Day the Elder and the Younger, Denomie's title refers to another Leech Lake Ojibwe man named Hole-in-the-Day, who was arrested in 1898 in a bootlegging case. *Indians in North America* notes that Hole-in-the-Day "opposed many government policies, and some Ojibwe thought the arrest was political." Anton Treuer et al., eds., *Indian Nations of North America* (Washington, DC: National Geographic, 1986), 53.

The Noble Savage as Entrepreneur

Indian Gaming Success

Julie Pelletier

As a researcher who has studied American Indian casinos and gaming since 1994, I have encountered a narrow range of reactions to my work. Depending on the context, I may be asked about gaming and gambling as *sin*—this comes up primarily in the United States and, yes, in academic settings. The first time I encountered that question was during a job talk—I was so startled that I answered the question awkwardly, effectively eliminating the department's interest in hiring me. Or I'm asked for a pragmatic, cost-benefit analysis—"does gaming help tribes/bands/Indian people?" That question is easier for me to answer with some quick sound bites that, hopefully, counteract the pervasive misinformation on the subject. Sound bites are not going to convey the complexity of how or whether gaming is or can be positive, but when one is speaking against an overwhelmingly negative, under/misinformed backdrop of representation of Indigenous gaming, you do what you can! The other common response to my research is from academics, especially cultural anthropologists, and nonacademics alike—the fear, concern, or conviction that Indians are "losing their culture" by participating in gaming and running casinos. I refer to this as the Noble Savage dilemma, bringing to the forefront tensions over identity and authenticity.

33

This chapter will not focus on the concept of gaming and gambling as sin, because I see that question or concern as intertwined in the colonial and Christian worldview from which the Noble Savage myth is drawn. Various studies demonstrate the ubiquity of games of chance and betting activities in many North American Indigenous cultures precontact, thereby positioning moral evaluations of gaming activities in the postcontact context, and in the dynamic of assimilation. Early anthropologists, such as Lewis Henry Morgan, tended to interpret Indian gaming through the lens of ceremony or as a reflection of the laziness and inferiority of Indian peoples. Yale Belanger argues that focusing on Indigenous gaming's ceremonial and religious importance "obscures insights into the nature of historic North American Indigenous gaming, specifically the centrality of gaming to Indigenous political economy. Reliance upon narrow categories hampers our ability to appreciate how gaming informed complex political and economic ideologies and practices."[1] I carry forward Belanger's argument by addressing the latter two reactions I've encountered—the interest in a cost-benefit analysis, and the Noble Savage versus Rich Indian dynamic.

In this chapter I examine contradictions between perceptions of Indians as successful entrepreneurs and as Noble Savages—contradictions that can reflect tension over nation-building efforts by tribes—through a study of how municipalities are putting revenue-sharing monies to use.[2] During fieldwork among the Sault Ste. Marie Tribe in the mid-1990s, I examined tribal identity, focusing on the strategic use of ritual by various age and interest groups in the tribe.[3] While my primary focus was not on Indian gaming, I was aware that its impact on identity was considerable and has only become more so in the ensuing years. With this in mind, I returned to the Upper Peninsula (UP) of Michigan in 2008 to interview public officials regarding the impact of Indian gaming on local municipalities, particularly as it relates to revenue-sharing.[4] I am also interested in contributing to research on Indian gaming and casinos that is based on fieldwork and other types of quantitative and qualitative research. Much of what is presented and published on the topic is not supported by research.[5]

My chapter begins with an introduction to the image of the Noble Savage. I provide an examination of the economic success of tribes in the UP, particularly the Soo Tribe (the tribe's commonly used nickname), and I provide a brief historical context of the Soo Tribe and an overview of its economic development. I then consider the implications of this success in a larger context: essentialist assumptions about American Indians that conflict with perceptions of them as entrepreneurs with capitalist goals and values. Also of interest are the ways in which mandated revenue-sharing is put to use by municipalities. My research details for what projects and purposes municipalities are requesting funding as well as what applications are approved by tribes. This case study, which includes comparative analysis of changes in attitudes and perceptions toward Indian entrepreneurship from the 1990s to the present among public officials whose municipalities are affected by Indian gaming and other economic development, reveals both changing and persistent perceptions of Indian peoples.

The Tenacity of the Noble Savage Image

The image of the Noble Savage is tenacious and pervasive, influencing media and scholarly analyses and representations of Indigenous peoples, particularly in relation to economic activities. I argue that the Soo Tribe's Indigenous identity (and that of other economically successful tribes) has been attacked in part because its financial acumen challenges people's understanding of what it means to be Indian and because the representation of itself as a nation raises concerns about U.S. nationalism. Like many contemporary Indian tribes, the Soo Tribe finds itself caught in dilemmas of representation and of identity.

The rapid growth of Indian gaming has also sparked controversies over who exactly is an Indian and what exactly qualifies as an Indian nation. Some of this controversy is the result of mainstream society's stereotyping, which often sees "Indian" in terms of images in which Indigenous peoples are not "supposed" to engage in capitalistic business enterprises or thrive economically in contemporary modes.[6]

The Noble Savage has no interest in economic development—he or she is at one with Nature and is not driven by economic interests. She or he is naive and innocent, honest to a fault, and ignorant. How can such a person run a multimillion-dollar enterprise while wading through layers of bureaucratic red tape (or "white tape," as an elder termed it) required by the U.S. government? Ronald Niezen positions indigenism in relation to colonization and nationalizing projects that sought and seek to erase difference, especially difference that comes with sovereignty claims.[7] Fears of internal dissent, possibly leading to secession, can and have led to acts of ethnocide and genocide aimed at Indigenous peoples. The process of assimilation into the dominant culture involves the use of the tools of education and religion to create a hegemonic subclass.[8] When the Native appears to be properly subdued and well on his or her way to being assimilated, a wave of nostalgia sweeps over the colonizers, and the ideal of the Noble Savage takes hold of the imagination. Indians and other Indigenous peoples are seen, according to Niezen, as "represent[ng] an alternative, a form of life based on patience, simple goals, and suspension of temporal imperatives."[9] It is frightening to be "foreign," "alien," or "other"—it is really cool to be "alternative." The stereotype of Indigenous peoples as inherently and essentially lacking in economic skills and interests reflects the romantic ideals placed on them by the dominant culture and can serve to paralyze economic development as envisioned by tribal communities.

Economic development in American Indian communities, as well as for many other Indigenous peoples, is also constrained by policy and legislation, and this chapter does not mean to ignore or diminish the significance of policy. However, reigning attitudes, such as a belief in Indigenous peoples as Noble Savages, affect the political will, as can be seen in the pendulum swing of American Indian policy—policy is not written and applied in a vacuum. So my analysis includes an understanding of the role of policy whether stated explicitly or not, but of policy as understood in a cultural context. The following section places the economic development of the Soo Tribe in historical context, identifying key factors that allow, encourage, or limit the tribe's activities.

Historical Background

The Wheeler-Howard Act of 1934 set goals for tribes and bands to move toward self-governance and "for tribal organizations to be chartered as federal corporations."[10] Encouraged by this new philosophy, tribal elders in Sault Ste. Marie began the tedious process of compiling the necessary documentation to apply for federal tribal recognition. At the same time, the city of Sault Ste. Marie was growing and prospering, but no improvements were made in the Indian part of town, which centered on Marquette Avenue and Shunk Road. The Mar Shunk neighborhood, as it is known, featured poor housing built on swampy land, unpaved roads so poor that school buses would not pick up the children, and no water or sewer services.[11]

Soo Tribal Recognition and Development

In 1972, the Soo Tribe was accorded federal recognition. This status brought empowerment, which it exercised almost immediately, successfully suing the City of Sault Ste. Marie over the spending of a Community Development Block Grant, none of which was to be used for improvements to the Mar Shunk neighborhood.[12] More than a decade later, the Soo Tribe began its successful foray into gaming. Like many tribes, it began with one bingo hall; its largest casino complex now encompasses 80,000 square feet. The Soo Tribe manages its own casinos and has provided consultants for other tribes wishing to do the same. Michigan Consultants, a firm based in Lansing, conducted an economic impact study of the Soo Tribe's casinos in 2007. At that time, they listed gross revenues for five casinos at $123.9 million.[13] The Soo Tribe does not participate in formal revenue-sharing or per capita payments to its membership but instead spends more than 90 percent of revenues on services such as health care, housing, and education.[14]

The Soo Tribe has purchased land for housing, businesses, and member services, focusing on housing, health care, social services, employment, and education. It acquired a former air force base, which, in addition to tribal housing, contains hangars, warehouses, and a day care center. It owns two other housing facilities and runs several day care centers. Health care is another priority. In 1995, the Tribe opened a health center in Sault Ste. Marie. The Rural Health Service was developed, and several smaller clinics were built. A partnership with the University of Michigan and a local hospital led to the construction of a new hospital in St. Ignace, a city in the tribe's service area. The Tribe also owns and operates a K–12 charter school in cooperation with the State of Michigan. In addition, it provides college scholarships and encourages members in college to apply for internships with the tribe in a variety of areas. The tribe's social services and court system often works as a critical buffer between the dominant culture's social services and legal institutions, advocating for tribal members and administering programs and enforcing rules according to the Soo Tribe's codes and constitution.

Cultural preservation efforts are also supported with casino revenues. For example, lodges are built next to the community centers for traditional functions such as ceremonies, free Anishinabe language classes are available, and tribal members are offered opportunities to learn or share in drumming, dancing, and traditional crafts. An annual powwow serves to gather many of the far-flung members together. A cultural resource management office works on repatriation efforts, while another office has an ongoing oral history project. For many of the tribe's elders, the opportunity to speak their language and to participate in rituals openly brings them great joy, which is important in a tribal community with a strong cultural value placed on elders.

Tribal Identity and Ritualization

Transformed by sudden wealth and a rapid increase in membership due to the decision to define membership based on lineal descent (as opposed to blood quantum), the Soo Tribe worked in the 1990s to create or maintain a sense of tribal cohesiveness and identity.[15] Its efforts included the use of ritual as a strategic practice, or ritualization.[16] Ritualization was expressed through the strategic use of ritual to educate both insider tribal members and outsiders about Soo Tribe identity and to express and reinforce the Tribe's status as a sovereign entity. I will refer in this chapter specifically to ritualization as implemented by the elected leadership of the Tribe, which I saw as a response to federal Indian policies that have eroded Indian sovereignty while vastly complicating Indian identity.[17]

In the 1990s, the elected leaders of the Soo Tribe had clear objectives regarding the public and tribal image of the Soo Tribe. They saw events such as the opening of a new tribal administration facility as an opportunity to communicate their version of the tribal image: progressive yet rooted in tradition. These potentially contradictory elements could be melded, sometimes awkwardly, in ceremonies that commemorated and celebrated chosen events. In ceremonies like "grand openings," ritual elements could be used in innovative ways, reinforcing the concept of a progressive tribe rooted in tradition. One Tribal member joked to me that there is not anything for which the elected leadership could not find a blessing. This comment revealed the ambiguity that some Tribal members felt about the elected leadership's ritual strategies. It was my sense that most traditionally oriented members were reluctant to openly criticize the elected leadership; criticism was expressed privately. Publicly, most traditionally oriented members either did not comment on the activities of the elected leadership or they praised the many projects the elected leaders chose to fund, such as language and cultural revitalization and retention projects that support the values and goals of the traditionally oriented members. It was also my impression that some traditionally oriented Tribal members recognized the pragmatic nature of the work their elected leaders were engaged in to help the tribe. The ritual activities were accepted by most in the tribe because the elected leaders' goals were seen as worthy and of benefit to all tribal members. Some traditions, such as the inauguration ceremony for new board members, have become part of the tribe's culture, an expression of the changing and active nature of a society.

Tribal Influence

Like each of the dozen or so highly successful gaming tribes in the United States— the preeminent example being the Mashantucket Pequots in Connecticut—the Soo Tribe comes under intense public scrutiny, rivalries and infighting between political factions playing out in the press.[18] Also, the potential influence of the Soo Tribe is evident in the frequent visits made by politicians and business leaders to meet with tribal officials. In the past, it was beneath notice, but now the tribe is visited by political candidates. An undated U.S. Senate memo on campaign spending refers specifically to the Soo Tribe: "According to a DNC [Democratic National Committee] document, the Sault Ste. Marie Chippewas [*sic*] contributed a total of $282,500 to twelve different state Democratic parties" during the 1996 election cycle.[19] Tribal elections are followed carefully in the local media, reflecting an acute awareness of the effect the tribal elections and subsequent economic decisions may have on the non-Indian municipalities within its seven-county service area. The irony of this attention is not lost on the tribe, but neither are the implications of its new wealth. Similar dynamics occur in relation to the other gaming tribes in the UP—the Soo Tribe is simply the most significant example due to the tribe's preeminence in the gaming industry and to its large membership.

Gaming Compacts and Legal Challenges

The regulation of Indians demonstrates the influence of perceptions of Indians as Noble Savages lacking entrepreneurial interest and skills and needing the oversight of multiple governmental entities in their economic development projects. All of the federally recognized UP tribes, including the Soo Tribe, signed gaming compacts with the State of Michigan in 1993.[20] As part of the compact agreement, these tribes "are required to make semi-annual two percent (2%) payments directly to local units of government."[21] Four tribes also make 8 percent payments, which are paid directly into a state fund called the Michigan Strategic Fund; as part of a land agreement, all of the 1993 compact tribes except for the Keweenaw Band Indian Community ceased making 8 percent payments in 1998.[22] Gaming compacts negotiated after the 1996 *Seminole v. Florida* case often specify revenue-sharing arrangements and sometimes gaming exclusivity agreements.[23] States that have chosen to sign gaming compacts are placed in the position of negotiating with sovereignties—tribes and other American Indian entities—and, at times, behave badly because the stakes are local and the control is in the hands of state governments. The following court cases involving gaming compacts in Michigan illustrate tensions that often ensue between tribal and state governments. In both cases, the plaintiff is the State of Michigan, with Governor Jennifer Granholm representing the interests of the citizens of her state.

Sault Ste. Marie Tribe, et al. v. Granholm, 475 F.3d 805 (6d Cir. 2007), was heard in the U.S. Court of Appeals and represents a decision in favor of several Michigan gaming tribes. The suit involved the use of "comps" by Indian casinos.[24] Gaming tribes in Michigan have computed their net revenue without comps contributing to the gross revenue. The State of Michigan sued the Hannahville Indian Community, a UP tribe, to force the Tribe—and inevitably, other gaming tribes in Michigan that use comps as promotional tools—to assign a value to the comps, thereby increasing their revenues and, of course, their 2 percent payments to local governments. The U.S. Court of Appeals' decision requires the district court to consider extrinsic evidence produced by the Hannahville Indian Community supporting the tribe's argument that comps are part of the broader gaming industry's common practice and are calculated as a revenue loss.

In this case, the tribe won through the appeals process the right to be evaluated according to the standards and practices established by the Nevada Gaming Commission and American Institute of Public Accountants Audit and Accounting Guide for Casinos. The case is interesting in that it reveals the sometimes draconian standards to which Indian gaming enterprises are held, in comparison to private gaming corporations, as well as the intense interest state governments have in closely monitoring Indian gaming.

Another court case involving Indian gaming in Michigan ended in a settlement between Governor Granholm and two tribes in the lower peninsula of Michigan concerning state-sponsored keno.[25] The Little River Band of Ottawa Indians and the Little Traverse Bands of Ottawa Indians suspended 8 percent payments to the state when the Michigan Lottery introduced Club Keno, citing this action as a violation of the 1998 gaming compact, which was supposed to guarantee the tribes protection from gaming competition. The state filed suit, and the settlement agreement announced March 21, 2008, spells out, among other conditions, a definition of gaming exclusivity as no longer being measured on a statewide basis, and an agreement by these tribes to reduce their contributions to the state from 8 percent to 6 percent.[26] The long-term implications of this settlement could be far-reaching and bear continued attention.

Two Percent Payments in the UP

After fifteen years, tribal distributions of 2 percent payments to surrounding municipalities have become bureaucratized and routine. Each tribe decides how to handle the distribution; most tribes in the UP now accept applications biannually from local governments to fund particular projects or to cover specific expenses. At least one tribe, the Bay Mills Indian Community, does not have an application process, so it does not designate how its 2 percent monies are spent by the municipalities in its service area. This unusual practice by the Bay Mills Tribe may be in part because this tribe has a small impact area—its two casinos are located in one county, for example, as compared to the Soo Tribe's six casinos located in four counties.

The tribes that use an application process do not approve all requests. Some local governments respond to the competitive nature of the process by prioritizing their multiple applications. Others do not. I know of at least one instance in which the Soo Tribe has requested that a government prioritize its applications. The municipal government refused because prioritizing applications is not part of the tribe's official application process. It is my impression, however, that most municipalities will accede to any reasonable request made by the tribes concerning the application process. The Hannahville Indian Community additionally requires six-month follow-up reports from the grantee detailing how and if objectives of the 2 percent grant proposal were met.[27]

My survey and interview data indicates that local governments regularly request funding in the area of public safety. A city or township may request 2 percent monies for an ambulance or as matching funds toward a fire truck. In 2006, for example, the Soo Tribe purchased an ambulance for Kinross Charter Township and a water tanker truck for Bruce Township, contributing almost $74,000 for those two requests alone. Additional ancillary equipment and supplies for fire, ambulance, and other emergency services can be more difficult to write into federal grant applications, and tribes have been willing to either match or fund these purchases. Officials in Escanaba, located in Delta County, offered an example when I interviewed them. The Delta County Sheriff's Office was able to purchase a personal water craft using 2 percent monies from the Hannahville Indian Community, a purchase that was not without controversy as some community and tribal members questioned the utility of what is essentially defined as a recreational vehicle. The controversy disappeared after a deputy rescued a near-drowning victim using the Jet Ski.

Multiple factors play into municipalities' requests for funding in the area of public safety. Geographic isolation is one factor—it can take an ambulance or fire truck twenty minutes or more to respond to a call for help from outlying communities, so residents will want that emergency vehicle to be as fully equipped as possible. Municipalities in the UP, affected by a sluggish economy in an area known historically for its boom-and-bust cycles, have often been unable to fund more than the minimum needed for public safety. Turning to the revenue-sharing dollars available from local tribes has proven highly advantageous for both the municipalities, which benefit directly, and for tribes, who gain not only increased public safety for their members and casino visitors but also positive publicity. As one municipal official noted, "If it's something you can take a picture of, it's a good item to ask for" (January 16, 2008; Escanaba, Michigan).

Other requests from municipalities include support for recreational facilities such as community centers and parks and recreational programming, especially for youth. Again, we can see mutual benefits for tribal and nontribal residents who use the facilities and programming. Additional recreational requests are meant for projects that will serve tourists as well as local residents, such as grooming equipment for snowmobile trails. Heritage projects, such as museums and cultural programming, are also supported by tribal revenue-sharing dollars, and will serve both tourists and local residents. An example of this is the Museum of Ojibwa Culture, formerly the Old St. Ignace Museum, in St. Ignace, Michigan.

A topic that came up repeatedly as I interviewed municipal officials was the practice of "pass-through." "Pass-through" is a term used to describe the funneling of 2 percent monies through municipal governments to nongovernmental organizations. According to the Michigan gaming compacts, 2 percent payments are to be made only to governmental entities. According to the Michigan Department of Treasury, municipalities are not allowed to make charitable donations to nonprofit

TABLE 1. Eight Percent Payments to Michigan Strategic Fund by Sault Ste. Marie Tribe of Chippewa Indians

August 20, 1993–September 30, 1994	$3,811,159.31
October 1, 1994–September 30, 1995	$7,633,353.52
October 1, 1995–September 30, 1996	$7,801,197.90
October 1, 1996–September 30, 1997	$7,480,181.21
October 1, 1997–September 30, 1998	$8,067,339.54
October 1, 1998–June 30, 1999	$5,884,340.48
Total	*$40,677,571.96*

Source: Michigan Gaming Control Board, 8% Payments to Michigan Strategic Fund (Michigan Economic Development Corporation), January 15, 2008, http://www.michigan.gov/documents/8_percent_Payments_76616_7.pdf.

TABLE 2. Two Percent Payments to Local Governments by Sault Ste. Marie Tribe of Chippewa Indians

August 20, 1993–September 30, 1994	$984,320.65
October 1, 1994–September 30, 1995	$1,710,403.44
October 1, 1995–September 30, 1996	$2,030,777.74
October 1, 1996–September 30, 1997	$1,851.505.38
October 1, 1997–September 30, 1998	$2,018,591.77
October 1, 1998–September 30, 1999	$2,114,801.36
October 1, 1999–September 30, 2000	$1,978,515.28
October 1, 2000–September 30, 2001	$2,004,083.79
October 1, 2001–September 30, 2002	$1,932,657.95
October 1, 2002–September 30, 2003	$1,913,192.02
October 1, 2003–September 30, 2004	$1,926,099.32
October 1, 2004–September 30, 2005	$1,960,728.67
October 1, 2005–September 30, 2006	$1,982,290.65
October 1, 2006–September 30, 2007	$1,951,245.52
October 1, 2007–September 30, 2008	$1,939,846.43
Total	*$28,299,078.97*

Source: Michigan Gaming Control Board, 2% Payments to Local Governments, June 29, 2009, http://www.michigan.gov/documents/2_percent_Payments_76617_7.pdf.

organizations: "This prohibition includes churches, veterans' organizations, community organizations, Little League, Boy Scouts, Big brothers/Big Sisters, etc."[28] Yet municipal governments in the UP regularly serve as pass-throughs for requests for 2 percent monies by charitable and nonprofit organizations. Only one municipal official I interviewed—Jason Oberle, then Kinross Township supervisor and chief executive official, and, coincidentally, Soo Tribe member—refused to approve pass-throughs, citing the state's lawful expenditures rule. Others expressed uneasiness about serving as pass-throughs but say they are pressured to continue a practice that often existed prior to their own tenure. At least one longtime public official has told a county auditor that he does not "give a damn about that" when warned about the illegality of pass-throughs. I am not aware of any legal challenges to the pass-through practice by the State of Michigan, which has otherwise seemed quick to file suits against tribes if the state fears its share of the Indian gaming profits will be affected.

The overall economic impact of mandated revenue-sharing is significant. Between 1993 and 1999, the Soo Tribe paid more than $40 million in 8 percent payments to the state (see table 1). As of December 31, 2008, communities in the UP received just under $58 million in 2 percent payments.[29] Of that, more than $28 million was paid by the Soo Tribe, which, on average, has paid close to $2 million annually in 2 percent payments since 1993 (see table 2). The irony of this arrangement is that tribes are providing services and materials for municipalities that are not provided by the federal government, the very entity that has chipped away at and intruded upon the sovereignty of the tribes.

Attitudes and Perceptions: The Noble Savage as Entrepreneur

Upon my return to the UP in 2008, I found that local government officials were much less likely to express incredulity at the ability of gaming tribes to be financially successful. Clearly fifteen years of revenue-sharing payments supplementing municipal budgets in the economically depressed UP had changed attitudes. There is also the possibility that those with negative attitudes toward tribal entrepreneurship have become more circumspect when being interviewed. In several cases the public officials I interviewed expressed concern that any negative comments they made to me might damage their relationships with the local tribes.

This concern about tribal perceptions and attitudes toward local municipalities is in striking contrast to interviews I conducted in this area in the 1990s, when several public officials spoke openly to me, with no expressed fear of repercussions, about their beliefs that "the Indians" were incapable of running successful businesses; at least one individual insisted that "the Indians" were not even capable of putting in a full day's work, so how could they be expected to run a casino? At the time of the earlier interviews—1994–1995—the local governments had received $2.69 million from the Soo Tribe alone in 2 percent payments. The other five gaming tribes in the UP, with smaller enterprises than the Soo Tribe, paid $1.49 million in 2 percent payments in 1994–1995, not an inconsiderable sum considering the economic state of the UP even then. At the present time, the only business that competes with the Soo Tribe as the largest employer in the UP is the prison system based in Kinross. One elected public official describes his relationship with the Soo Tribe thus:

> It is necessary for me to be able to work with whoever is chair of the tribe. As long as Aaron (Payment, who was tribal chair at the time of this interview) will take my calls and work with me, that's what counts. . . . You don't have to agree with everything they say or do. But the (municipality) needs to stay on good terms with whoever is making the decisions. (January 15, 2008)

Does political strategizing as demonstrated in the quote above reflect a new perspective on Indians or does it simply reflect a keen awareness of shifting power dynamics unrelated to indigenism or stereotypes about Indians? Certainly, there has been a shift in power or at least a dramatic increase in political and economic power for some tribes. In the 1990s, many observers of the Soo Tribe's phenomenal economic success expressed to me their surprise and even shock. This reaction was accompanied by questions about the tribe's authenticity and Indigenous identity.[30] The tribe was criticized for lacking in cultural knowledge, for having many members who are of mixed white and Indian ancestry, and for being too "white" in their business dealings—these criticisms came from tribal members, from other Michigan tribes, and from members of the dominant culture. The Tribal administration responded to some of these criticisms by hiring cultural consultants to increase cultural knowledge. They pointed out historical factors outside of Indian control that led to loss of land and language and traditions. Changes were made in the functioning of the Tribal enterprises, including casinos, to counter the criticism that administrative and other policies reflected the norms and values of the dominant culture rather than Ojibwa norms and values. For example, a process was instituted allowing Tribal members/employees to apply for cultural leaves to participate in traditional foraging activities or to attend ceremonies. The Tribal administration took action to situate themselves as traditionally and authentically grounded in Ojibwa culture while insisting on the tribe's right to pursue economic projects such as gaming.

Much of the world does not want to hear about visions of Indian economic development that include gaming and casinos.[31] Gaming strikes a sour note for many inside and outside of gaming tribes, particularly in conflict with Christian beliefs about sin and the evils of gambling. For others, the resistance to Indian gaming is influenced by perceptions of Indians as noncompetitive, as untouched and unsoiled by "filthy lucre"—in other words, as Noble Savages who are better off pursuing their "traditional" subsistence strategies of hunting, fishing, and simple gardening.[32] The Harvard Project on American Indian Economic Development's latest analysis points out that Indians are either left out of media coverage entirely or, as one study reports,[33] the coverage centers on "corrupt campaign practices, tying gaming operations to political contributions,"[34] with a recent example being the Jack Abramoff lobbying scandal. Light and Rand note that much of the media coverage of Indian gaming focuses on charges of factionalism, nepotism, corruption, and rumors of organized crime involvement.[35] They point out that lobbying funded by tribes, especially when tribes are competing for economic opportunities such as state approval to build a casino, meets with strong disapproval from the dominant culture.[36] Tribes publicizing their competing interests challenge the notion of a single unified Indian presence in the United States, with one culture, one experience, and one shared set of goals and interests.

What also clouds our understanding of Indian gaming is false representations of all gaming tribes as wildly successful, when most gaming tribes are only moderately profitable due to poor location, to competition for casino patrons, or to what Cornell and Kalt label "the standard approach to development of Native nations."[37] In the standard approach, the development agenda is set by outsiders; the focus is on short-term, nonstrategic "solutions"; and cultural diversity is seen as a barrier or impediment to economic success.[38] Tribal leaders in this approach are seen as redistributors of resources instead of as creative visionaries who lead the tribe in identifying and capitalizing on development opportunities that are consonant with tribal cultural values and goals. The mindset in the standard approach is survival—which leaves little or no room for planning, strategizing, and dreaming, critical components of what Cornell and Kalt call "the nation-building approach."[39]

The nation-building approach can arouse strong reactions as long-held assumptions about the proper relationship between tribes and the dominant culture are challenged. During my earlier fieldwork in the UP, I heard the Soo Tribe described repeatedly as "arrogant." One of the people who used this adjective in relation to the Soo Tribe was former mayor Bill Lynn of Sault Ste. Marie, who otherwise was quite supportive of the tribe's growing economic success, although he was not in favor of putting land into trust, an understandable reaction on his part when one considers that trust land cannot be taxed. In 1995, he had the following advice for the tribe:

> They must forget what happened in the past. They're getting an arrogant attitude from an [outside] advisor. The non-Native community understands how bad things were. It's time to move on. They must stop being so arrogant. They are part of the community and must act like it. [The tribe] could be such a positive element in the city. This would shut up the critics. (September 6, 1995)

Another vocal critic of the Soo Tribe, Verna Lawrence, described several times by former mayor Lynn as a "card-carrying Indian" and tribal member, also used the word "arrogant" when discussing the tribe's activities (September 19, 1995). She stated that "culture is dead in the Soo Tribe" and derided cultural revitalization attempts: "Will you give up central heat, etc. and go live in a teepee?"[40]

A self-described "American of Indian descent," Lawrence is politically conservative and, like most municipal officials, was concerned about land being put into trust and removed from the tax rolls. In 2008, it was clear from conversations with municipal officials that tribes recognize the increased burden their expansion and development can put on local infrastructures and have responded by making payments in lieu of taxes, a term commonly abbreviated as PILT. PILT is used to keep roads in good shape as well as providing up-to-date water and sewer and other municipal services to tribal members who live in local communities. Fears expressed in the early days of Indian casino development have proven unfounded as tribes voluntarily work out agreements to the mutual benefit of the tribes and the nontribal communities. Lawrence, like the mayor, called upon the Soo Tribe "to realize that they live in a community." By making PILT, gaming tribes in the UP demonstrate their responsibility and commitment to the larger communities in which they live.

The nation-building approach to development can arouse anxiety as tribal communities define themselves by pushing against state and federal systems and policies. Verna Lawrence provides an illustration of anxiety about her tribe's changing relationship with the State of Michigan:

> The [Soo] Tribe should not be so arrogant with the state [of Michigan]. The money should go to the people, not to political campaigns. [They] aren't politically astute. They could use the money for dental, eye care, ill members, burial of the dead. [It's an] Indian Mafia system of government.[41]

Much is revealed in the inflammatory rhetoric for which Lawrence is known. Like most, if not all, gaming tribes, the Soo Tribe did then and does now use casino profits for health care and burial benefits. The characterization of the Soo Tribe as not "politically astute" is particularly poignant coming from a member of the Soo Tribe who is the first and only Indian and first and only woman elected to the office of mayor in Sault Ste. Marie. She may understand her own political savvy as working within the dominant system, while the nation-building efforts of the Soo Tribe position them simultaneously as "arrogant" troublemakers working outside the system and as politically naive.

My sense is that Lawrence's reference to the Mafia (a reference I heard from other Indian and non-Indian community members in the 1990s) is a commentary on the frequently criticized practice of nepotism found in many, if not most, U.S. tribes, including the Soo Tribe. I found it fascinating to watch the Soo Tribe's Human Resources office move a difficult-to-place tribal member from job to job until the right placement was found for him, long after a typical American corporation would have terminated the person's employment. Adopting many characteristics of the dominant society's corporate culture includes adapting many characteristics of that culture to suit tribal values and norms, another characteristic of the nation-building approach to development. What is being read by some as either bad business practice or as corrupt or even criminal behavior—nepotism—may be seen as a traditional element of many Native communities. The introduction of gaming, with its negative associations with sin and crime, has influenced perceptions of particular cultural practices such as nepotism that either conflict with commonly accepted practices in the dominant culture or arouse suspicions of wrongdoing.

Brian Calliou, program director for the Banff Centre's Indigenous Leadership and Management programs, observes that "when Indians get successful, there can be a backlash."[42] For some tribes, countering negative backlash with publicity of their own can go against strongly held cultural norms. While I have seen efforts by the Dakota gaming communities in Minnesota to boost their public image, this strategy has been and continues to be distasteful to these tribes, particularly in revealing their charitable contributions.

The Soo Tribe was in its infancy concerning public relations in the 1990s, and I observed a sophisticated public relations campaign on my return in 2008. The tribe's response to the dilemmas of representation and of identity include (re) presenting itself as simultaneously progressive and traditional, and also includes the strategic use of rituals and ceremonies—ritualization—to place itself in the category of the sovereign indigenous.[43]

Public rituals and ceremonies situate the tribe, in some way, in the realm of the Noble Savage—the truly Indigenous—"noble, strong, spiritually wise, and, above all, environmentally discreet."[44] Efforts to communicate and enhance tribal identity through public ritual and ceremonies, and through public relations efforts that identify Indians as environmentalists or as existing in the past, can essentialize Indians, serving to perpetuate the Noble Savage stereotype. Niezen observes, "Even those states that strive toward pluralism and cultural tolerance find it difficult to go much beyond the accommodation of recreational diversity, the celebrations of differences through such things as sporting events, arts, and festivals."[45] "Recreational diversity" can be accommodated because it presents diversity as edutainment and is usually not intended to challenge societal norms. However, it is unclear if retaining ceremonies, rituals, and other spiritually based activities in the public relations toolbox of today's entrepreneurial tribes is a wise or efficacious strategy.

The authors of the latest Harvard study on American Indian economic development illustrate the tenacity of the romantic ideal of the Noble Savage in the imaginations of academics:

> As if economic development and Indianness were in inherent conflict, Chief [Philip] Martin was once asked by an audience of non-Indian university students what the phenomenal economic development at Mississippi Choctaw was doing to Choctaw culture. After contemplating the question, Chief Martin answered straightforwardly and with profound insight: "Well, it used to be that everyone moved away, but now they're all coming back."[46]

Chief Martin's statement gets to the root of the conflicting perceptions of Indian entrepreneurship. Economic development brings tribal members back;

provides training, education, and jobs for tribal members; and often supports cultural retention and revitalization efforts. If tribal members must leave the community for work, the tribal community and culture suffer, for culture lives in a society's members and can be lost when the members scatter. Yet many academics continue to fret about the effects of entrepreneurship and economic development on tribal cultures.

I presented an earlier version of this work at the joint meetings of Canadian and American anthropologists in Toronto in 2007, meetings that provided two examples of academic infatuation with the Noble Savage myth. The first came during the plenary address by John and Jean Comaroff, during which John objectified Native peoples, ridiculing their efforts to survive and, perhaps, even to prosper, despite hundreds of years of attempted physical and cultural genocide. I listened to chuckles and appreciative snorts from many anthropologists sitting in the auditorium as John wove his carefully and cleverly worded tale of Ethnicity, Inc. and made-up" American Indian "tribes" and "nations" with "traditions."[47]

Researchers working in Indian Country are aware that successful gaming and other economic development have exacerbated tensions and conflicts surrounding identity, tribal membership, and authenticity. What is irresponsible and inaccurate to leave out of an anthropological analysis of U.S. Indigenous identity politics, sovereignty claims, and cultural commodification, however, is a historically contextualized discussion of Indian policy.

The second day of the same conference provided yet another example of the tenacity of anthropologists' perceptions of Indian peoples as Noble Savages. After listening to several papers on Indian gaming (including mine), a sympathetic anthropologist who is active not only in academic work but also works in an applied capacity for Indian tribes expressed her concern that Indian gaming might harm "the [tribal] culture [sic],"[48] so the tribal members must "watch out" for that possibility. The myth of the Noble Savage continues to fuel resistance to recognizing tribal economic development as an expression of sovereignty, resistance, and resilience.

Continued research is needed to counteract the Noble Savage image as well as the newer but equally destructive Rich Indian image. Reflexive awareness of images and stereotypes that may affect our perceptions and analyses can be facilitated through community participation research, involving tribal members at every stage of the project. Of great importance also are the lived experiences and observations of those directly affected by Indian gaming. Jim Northrup, Anishinaabe writer and member of a Minnesota gaming tribe, provided keen and often humorous observations on the impact of casinos. He riffed on familiar themes of contemporary Indian life, including rez cars, commodity foods, and powwows. In a collection titled *Anishinaabe Syndicate: A View from the Rez*, Northrup provided a nuanced perspective on casinos, bingo, and economic development:

> What do they do with the profits from Big Bucks Bingo and Fond-du-Luth? Some smaller reservations are paying their members thousands a month from their casino and bingo operations. We just know there is a profit but we don't know where it goes.[49]
>
> The good part is that the casino is providing jobs. I have sisters, nieces, and cousins working there.[50]

While these two brief quotes are just a sample of Northrup's thoughts on casinos and gaming, they reflect the reality of the lived experience, which includes tensions over the ubiquity of gambling; concerns over financial transparency, economic development decision-making, and control; and even the incorporation of gaming as a cultural motif in humor and other cultural expressions. Research teams that draw upon the strengths, knowledge, and resources of community members and scholars from a variety of disciplines could provide valuable information, insights, and recommendations untainted by dehumanizing and politically and economically paralyzing caricatures of Indigenous peoples.

NOTES

This chapter would not have been possible without the following support. My doctoral research in the 1990s was funded through a research grant from the Sault Ste. Marie Tribe of Chippewa Indians and a King-Chavez-Parks Future Faculty Fellowship, the latter administered through the Department of Anthropology at Michigan State University. My return to the UP in 2008 was funded by a University of Minnesota, Morris Faculty Research Enhancement Fund grant. The University of Minnesota, Morris (UMM) supported my attendance at conferences where I presented versions of this work and received valuable comments from Becca Gercken, Darrel Manitowabi, and others. Zachary Firestone, while an undergraduate sociology student at UMM, provided assistance with survey data.

1. Yale Belanger, "Toward an Innovative Understanding of North American Indigenous Gaming in Historical Perspective," in *First Nations Gaming in Canada*, ed. Yale Belanger (Winnipeg: University of Manitoba Press, 2011), 10.

2. Earlier versions of this work were presented at the joint meetings of the Canadian Anthropological Society and the American Ethnological Association in Toronto, May 2007, and the American Anthropological Association meetings in San Francisco, November 2008.

3. Julie Pelletier, "The Role of Ritual in a Contemporary Ojibwa Tribe" (PhD diss., Michigan State University, 2002).

4. The first set of interviews referred to in this chapter was conducted with only nontribal public officials due to a delay in gaining University of Minnesota Institutional Review Board (IRB) ethics approval to interview tribal officials and individuals. I inadvertently interviewed two Sault Ste. Marie tribal members who also happened to be elected municipal officials, a circumstance unanticipated by the University of Minnesota IRB.

5. Jean Comaroff and John L. Comaroff, *Ethnicity, Inc.* (Chicago: University of Chicago Press, 2009), is an example of an opinion piece, while Steven Andrew Light and Kathryn R. L. Rand, *Indian Gaming and Tribal Sovereignty: The Casino Compromise* (Lawrence: University Press of Kansas, 2005); Yale Belanger, ed., *First Nations Gaming in Canada* (Winnipeg: University of Manitoba Press, 2011); Mark Manitowabi, *The Governing of Indian Reserves Authorities of the Band under the Indian Act* (Ottawa: Department of Indian Affairs and Northern Development, 1980); and Jessica R. Cattelino, *High Stakes: Florida Seminole Gaming and Sovereignty* (Durham, NC: Duke University Press, 2008) all base their analyses on research.

6. Harvard Project on American Indian Economic Development, *The State of Native Nations: Conditions under U.S. Policies of Self-Determination* (New York: Oxford University Press, 2008), 154.

7. Ronald Niezen, *The Origins of Indigenism: Human Rights and the Politics of Identity* (Berkeley: University of California Press, 2003).

8. Duane Champagne, "Rethinking Native Relations," in *Indigenous Peoples and the Modern State*, ed. D. Champagne, K. J. Torjesen, and S. Steiner (Walnut Creek, CA: Alta Mira Press 2005); Marie Battiste, "Introduction," in *Reclaiming Indigenous Voice and Vision*, ed. M. Battiste (Vancouver: University of British Columbia Press, 2000); Linda Tuhiwai Smith, *Decolonizing Methodologies: Research and Indigenous Peoples* (Dunedin, New Zealand: Zed Books, 1999).

9. Niezen, *Origins of Indigenism*, 178.

10. Edmund Jefferson Danziger Jr., *The Chippewas of Lake Superior* (Norman: University of

Oklahoma Press, 1979), 134.

11. Charles E. Cleland, *Rites of Conquest: The History of Michigan's Native Americans* (Ann Arbor: University of Michigan Press, 1992).

12. This account is not only the Soo Tribe's version of events surrounding the block grant episode, but is widely accepted by others as well, such as Cleland, *Rites of Conquest*, 279. However, it is not uncontested. Verna Lawrence, former member of the Soo Tribe board as well as former city council member, stated that "the League of Women Voters got water and sewer on Mar Shunk, not the tribe. The tribe never lifted a finger, including [Joe] Lumsden." Interview, Sault Ste. Marie, Michigan, September 19, 1995.

13. Light and Rand, *Indian Gaming and Tribal Sovereignty*, note that much of the research conducted on the economic impact of Indian gaming has been done by private think tanks.

14. The Soo Tribe does not participate in formal revenue-sharing or per capita payments to its membership but instead spends its net revenues on services such as health care, housing, and education.

15. Tribal membership increased dramatically after 1975 and is now approximately 44,000.

16. Catherine Bell, *Ritual Theory, Ritual Practice* (New York: Oxford University Press, 1992).

17. In my dissertation, I analyze ritualization as practiced by several subgroups or components of the tribe, including traditionally and nontraditionally oriented members of various age groups. Pelletier, "Role of Ritual."

18. The Pequots are referenced by most Indian gaming researchers as well as by the general media.

19. U.S. Senate Report, "DNC Efforts to Raise Money in the Indian Gaming Community," http://concepts.gslsolutions.com/gov/senate/hsgac/public/_archive/22.pdf. The report is undated but is likely from 1997 when the Senate was investigating Democratic National Congress spending during the 1996 election.

20. Specifically, Bay Mills Indian Community, Sault Ste. Marie Tribe of Chippewa Indians, Keweenaw Bay Indian Community, Lac Vieux Desert Band of Lake Superior Chippewa Indians, and Hannahville Indian Community. The other four gaming tribes in the UP have six casinos among them. There are twelve federally recognized tribes in Michigan.

21. "Tribal Casino Slot Revenue Payments & Slot Information," Michigan Gaming Control Board, http://www.michigan.gov. As part of the Indian Gaming Regulatory Act, "Congress delegated power to the states to regulate casino-style gaming—in its view, a clear and perhaps necessary compromise between state power and tribal sovereignty, but in the view of many tribes, a clear compromise of tribal sovereignty." Light and Rand, *Indian Gaming and Tribal Sovereignty*, 6.

22. The tribes making 8 percent payments to the State of Michigan in 2009 are the Keweenaw Bay Indian Community, the Little River Band of Ottawa Indians, and the Pokagon Band of Potawatomi Indians. The Match-E-Be-Nash-She-Wish Band of Pottawatomi Indians has not yet opened its first casino and will be required to make 8 percent and 2 percent payments. The Nottawaseppi Huron Band of Potawatomi is not required to make 2 percent payments to local governments, only the 8 percent to the state. The Nottawaseppi Huron Band of the Potawatomi, as of 2017, has contributed more than $107 million to the State of Michigan ("Press Room," FireKeepers Casino, http://www.firekeeperscasino.com/news). The Little Traverse Bay Bands of Odawa Indians has amended its compact with Michigan twice, successfully suing to reduce its revenue sharing to 6 percent. The State of Michigan provides the text of the compacts and amendments online: "Tribal-State Compacts," Michigan Gaming Control Board, http://www.michigan.gov.

23. See Cattelino, *High Stakes*, for a detailed discussion of the case.

24. Comps—an abbreviation of "complementary"—are free game coupons or tokens intended to encourage casino visitors to gamble.

25. Keno is a bingolike game offered at many casinos.

26. Tim Martin, "Tribes, Michigan Settle Gaming Revenue Dispute," *Indian Country Today*, April 16, 2008, www.indiancountrymedianetwork.com.

27. "2% Grant Information," Hannahville Indian Community, Band of Potawatomi, www.hannahville.net.

28. State of Michigan Department of Treasury, "Appendix H," in *State of Michigan Department of Treasury Audit Manual for Local Units of Government* (Rev. February 2012).

29. As of 2016, the total paid out was more than $437 million.

30. Becca Gercken-Hawkins refers to this as the "authenticity debate" in her analysis of the rhetoric surrounding American Indian identity. Becca Gercken-Hawkins, "Authentic Reservations: The Rhetorical War for Native American Identity" (PhD diss., University of Miami, Coral Gables, 2001). I am interested in the authenticity debate and its implications for education as well as its implications related to economic development. See Julie Pelletier and Becca Gercken, "The 'Old Ways' as New Methods: Decolonizing and Native Values in Academia," *Studies in the Humanities* 33, no. 2 (2006): 245–63, for a discussion of the authenticity debate and pedagogy. See Pelletier with McMurrin (2009) for a discussion of questions of authenticity when taking students into so-called postcolonial communities for off-campus study (*Re*)*locating the Postcolony: Implications and Complications of Off-Campus Study* Newcastle upon Tyne: Cambridge Scholars Publishing.

31. A nongaming example that demonstrates the application of the Noble Savage myth in a symbolically powerful context—that of the environment—comes from Niezen, who worked with the James Bay Cree in northern Quebec as they struggled with a hydroelectric megaproject that profoundly changed their way of life. Niezen notes that the emphasis was on publicizing the environmental and cultural catastrophe this dam project represented for the Cree but that no attention was given to the need for a new subsistence strategy now that their hunting, fishing, and trapping grounds were destroyed. Niezen, *Origins of Indigenism*, 182. The only realistic alternative for the tribe "lies in resource extraction from their territory, the timber and minerals coveted by outside 'developers.'" Niezen goes on to note that "these are not the kind of visions the outside world wants to hear about. Indians are supposed to protect and maybe even worship or communicate with trees; they are not supposed to sell lumbering and mineral extraction contracts to usually non-Indian companies." Ibid.

32. Many tribes practiced some form of gambling prior to and after contact, including betting on contests of strength or other accomplishments, and enjoying games of chance. Competition certainly was part of many tribes' values and practices as well.

33. Masaki Hidaka, *Media Coverage of Native Gaming Ventures: An Analysis of National and Regional Trends and Prescriptions for Improvement* (Cambridge, MA: Harvard University John F. Kennedy School of Government, April 1998).

34. Harvard Project on American Indian Economic Development, *State of Native Nations*, 310.

35. Light and Rand, *Indian Gaming and Tribal Sovereignty*.

36. Ibid.

37. Stephen Cornell and Joseph P. Kalt, "Two Approaches to the Development of Native Nations: One Works, the Other One Doesn't," in *Rebuilding Native Nations: Strategies for Governance and Development*, ed. M. Jorgensen (Tucson: University of Arizona Press, 2008), 7. I am applying this approach relatively uncritically in this chapter but am aware that the Cornell and Kalt approach is rightly criticized for ignoring policy implications, among other weaknesses.

38. Ibid., 7–8.

39. Ibid., 19.

40. Larry Nesper, incorrectly referring to Verna Lawrence as "Vera Lawrence," reports that she attended a rally against Ojibwa spearfishing at Lac du Flambeau in Minnesota—the rally took place in 1986. Nesper notes that "Vera Lawrence's claim that treaties were made with the full bloods, eliding the difference between politics and genetics, was repeated in the area until at least 1992. She was one of a few Indian people nationwide

to join with non-Indians in calling for the abrogation of treaties and the termination of the trust relationship between the bands and the federal government." Larry Nesper, *The Walleye War: The Struggle for Ojibwe Spearfishing and Treaty Rights* (Lincoln: University of Nebraska Press, 2002), 215.

41. Ibid.

42. Brian Calliou, "Discussion of Culture and Economics," in Champagne, Torjesen, and Steiner, *Indigenous Peoples and the Modern State*, 91.

43. Pelletier, "Role of Ritual"; Julie Pelletier, "Ritual Ceremony in a Contemporary Anishinabe Tribe," Working Paper Series (Morris: University of Minnesota, Morris, 2003). My theoretical perspective draws from Catherine Bell's work in religious studies, *Ritual Theory, Ritual Practice*; Victor Turner's work on ritual and performance, *The Anthropology of Performance* (New York: PAJ Publication, 1992); and Barbara Myerhoff's work on constructed ritual, "We Don't Wrap Herring in a Printed Page: Fusion, Fictions and Continuity in Secular Ritual," in *Secular Ritual*, ed. S. F. Moore and B. G. Myerhoff (Amsterdam: Van Gorcum, Assen, 1977), and *Number Our Days* (New York: E. P. Dutton, 1979).

44. Niezen, *Origins of Indigenism*, 186.

45. Ibid.

46. Harvard Project on American Indian Economic Development, *State of Native Nations*, 112.

47. I have inserted quotation marks to indicate where John Comaroff was using "air quotes" during his address in 2007. The Comaroffs' paper led to the publication of *Ethnicity, Inc.*

48. The "*sic*" after "culture" is purposeful and meant to draw attention to an anthropologist referring to tribal culture in the singular. There are tribal *cultures*—with many variations and differences. While this may seem like a petty difference, note that the United Nations Declaration on the Rights of Indigenous Peoples was delayed for years over the question of "people" versus "peoples." An anthropologist should have known better than to ignore or erase the differences.

49. Jim Northrup, *Anishinaabe Syndicate: A View from the Rez* (Minneapolis: Minnesota Historical Society, 2011), 34.

50. Ibid., 77.

(Re)Imagining First Nations Casinos

A Necessary Response to Ensure Economic Development

Yale D. Belanger

I n recent years First Nations casino operations in Canada have settled into predictable operational patterns.[1] Apart from the negligence that temporarily plagued the Saskatchewan Indian Gaming Authority (SIGA) in the early 2000s,[2] the seventeen national for-profit First Nations casinos are accomplished employers that maintain a relatively low profile. They produced more than $1 billion for Aboriginal development between 1996 and 2010.[3] For many, this period represented the peak of a turbulent political journey that began in the early 1980s when Manitoba and Ontario First Nations leaders approached their respective provincial host governments about constructing reserve casinos; and Saskatchewan leaders visited several American Indian casino operations to gather information. Observers from various facets of Canadian society immediately questioned the suitability of permitting First Nations to operate casinos, especially those that were perceived to be lacking social, economic, and political capital. The media likewise appraised the anticipated hardships associated with introducing a potentially harmful product into similarly portrayed dysfunctional First Nations. Federal officials declared that provincial governments were unauthorized to negotiate casino compacts with First Nations while bureaucrats at all levels expressed fears that authorizing reserve casino operations would be judged as yielding to Aboriginal race-based rights.[4] The gravity of the situation was not lost on First Nations leaders who were confronting a touchy public relations issue and grappling with a murky legal landscape that offered little clarity concerning the Aboriginal right to control reserve gambling. Notably all of these events occurred prior to any First Nation tabling a formal casino proposal.

The act of seeking out—or in this case identifying—potential alternative economic prospects (casinos) to stimulate reserve development engendered substantial push back from various circles. First Nations leaders pursuing the idea of constructing reserve casinos realized quickly that they would need to reconcile these various forces to achieve their goals. What they failed to realize is that, despite the proclaimed Canadian desire to see First Nations generate their own source revenue vis-à-vis innovative economic development projects, non-Aboriginal leaders had yet to fully accept Aboriginal peoples as contemporary economic agents. That is, federal officials favored farming, agriculture, local commercial ventures, and light industry as the basis for reserve development—any projects that fell outside the scope of these categories were not recognized. As historical geographer Frank Tough argues in his superb essay "From the Original 'Affluent Society' to the 'Unjust Society,'" this disconnect can be traced to the fur trade, which many writers have concluded was a universally enriching experience typified by freedom of choice and collective economic achievement.[5] Tough challenges this orthodoxy by suggesting that such arguments obscure the "racial division of labor [as] a key means for structuring the industry" that led to the "the relative proportion of income to each of the racial groups," thus influencing "their long-run social futures." He explains that "the mixed economy could not absorb commercial value in a manner that would fund future growth," and the resulting "inability of Native trappers to obtain more than a subsistence share of the fur industry's wealth has implications for trends in economic history."[6]

This process, in his opinion, set "Whites and Natives on different historical trajectories," resulting in significant economic imbalances that, over time, came to be institutionalized. Thus from both operational and ideological perspectives Canada's economic development was and remains in part based on the economic exploitation of Indigenous peoples.[7] Tough convincingly argues that the forced economic and social marginalization characteristic of the fur trade is evident in the contemporary polarized economic outcomes that frequently distinguish modern reserve economies from those of non-Indigenous communities. Reserve economies persist on society's economic fringes with limited opportunities for fruitful economic integration despite professed federal and increasingly frequent provincial desires to expand Aboriginal economic outcomes.[8] Non-Aboriginal Canadians remain relatively ignorant of these historic processes, and tend to blame Aboriginal economic inertia on an internal failure to adapt to modern economic principles. In this setting those First Nations that attempt economic development projects that both fall outside the realm of tradition (for example, hunting and gathering) and simultaneously fail to adhere to "modern" modes of production (for example, agriculture, ranching, or natural resource utilization) provoke a destabilizing sense of liminality that challenges Canadian attitudes reliant on stereotypes that reinforce a collective understanding of what First Nations are from an economic perspective (farmers and/or ranchers, not casino owners).

Resonating with several Supreme Court of Canada Aboriginal rights decisions, First Nations economic development remains frozen in time: society and its respective Indian policy envision First Nations as little more than maturing farmers and ranchers living and working in reserve communities. Yet it is within this context that First Nations, in the 1990s, managed to convince provincial officials in Alberta, Saskatchewan, and Ontario that they could successfully manage large, corporate casino operations. How precisely did they accomplish this feat, especially considering that the various governments' responses to these early demands were frequently antagonistic and grounded in a non-Aboriginal belief in how First Nations should economically develop? Further, what steps were taken in each province that led to a positive negotiated outcome? A similarity of responses is evident in each of the three provinces, which can then be evaluated to illustrate how First Nations leaders tailored their public persona to open up new economic development opportunities vis-à-vis reserve casinos. But at what points did these leaders reflect on their strategies and alter them in response to internal and extracommunity concerns? Perhaps most important, what concessions did First Nations leaders accept in return for gaining the ability to operate reserve casinos?

My reading of the primary and secondary resources indicates that three specific approaches to securing the right to construct and operate reserve casinos developed, and each is explored to aid in determining how First Nations adapted their public image in response to governmental and, to a lesser extent, public resistance to casino development: Aboriginal rights challenges in the form of assertive, potentially violent, and, by all government accounts, illegal attempts to operate casinos outside of provincial jurisdiction; Aboriginal rights claims that compelled federal officials to respond to First Nations' legal challenges citing their self-governing authority to operate reserve casinos; and negotiations with provincial agents seeking to legally secure the right to operate reserve casinos according to provincial regulation. Prior to engaging the following analysis, it is important to briefly trace the history of Aboriginal-newcomer interface to highlight strategic Aboriginal responses to a colonial process that severed two peoples' economic trajectories and forced Indigenous peoples to maintain historical efforts at political and economic adaptation in an effort to challenge Canadian hegemony.

Strategic Aboriginal Interface

Written within decades of the first extended First Nation–European contact, European leaders had come to accept John Locke's 1651 depiction of Indians as "the savage people of America" as normative. Yet in North America during this period First Nations and non-Aboriginal leaders were engaged in what the philosopher James Tully described as learning the art of mutual recognition.[9] In these instances, First Nations' attempts to foster political contact reflected historic political, economic, and social processes to guarantee positive relationships with the newly arrived Europeans.[10] Early settlers to North America may have embraced the popular stereotype of "Indian as savage," but over time those working economically and militarily alongside powerful Indigenous neighbors would acknowledge this concept's limited practical utility.[11] As Jeremy Waldron has written, when two sides meet the goal is to "come to terms with one another, and set up, maintain, and operate the legal frameworks that [are] necessary to secure peace, resolve conflicts, do justice, avoid great harms, and provide some basis for improving the condition of life."[12] To be recognized "is to emerge from anonymity, to be seen and acknowledged for what you are," which (ostensibly) leads to equality being recognized and differences acknowledged.[13] As Tough illustrated in the context of economic relations, over time state-imposed norms would come to overwhelm and replace these negotiated frameworks, resulting in the fading of the First Nations' political influence and the need to adapt to a new and ever-evolving political landscape.[14]

First Nations' political, economic, and social adaptability was fundamental to maintaining influence and countering colonization's more egregious effects, which demanded negotiating with settlers. As the Royal Commission on Aboriginal Peoples final report of 1996 noted, "There was a long and rich history of treaty making among the Aboriginal nations of the Americas before the arrival of Europeans" that was "expanded to include European powers."[15] Absent any obligation to cede lands these treaty relationships were established to confirm a state of peace and to create bonds between parties that nurtured political, military, and economic stability.[16] First Nations were important military allies that encouraged Europeans to incorporate "elements of Aboriginal protocol in their alliance-making practices."[17] Cross-cultural economic relationships, according to Tough, also remained strong until the late eighteenth century, when settlers asserted self-government, thus altering intercultural trade and familiar kinship ties.[18] Following the War of 1812, settler governments were less inclined to interact politically with First Nations, who, after 1830, were acknowledged as wards to the colonial government's guardianship.[19]

Immediately following Confederation (1867), legislating on behalf of Indians became Canada's chosen avenue of political engagement, which required First Nations leaders to employ diverse engagement strategies in order to maintain political influence. One such strategy was to create political organizations to challenge European political and economic claims to First Nations lands and resources. Another was to petition the British courts for assistance.[20] Between 1870 and 1946 twenty-four separate and autonomous Native political organizations were created to stem the loss of political influence attributable to federal Indian legislation and policies.[21] Led primarily by younger men educated in English and Canadian political traditions, by the end of the twentieth century's first decade these organizational leaders had witnessed firsthand the Crown's distaste for political negotiations. By the 1940s, political organizing had grown to the point that Native leaders were invited to Ottawa in 1946 to testify before federal officials about Indian affairs administration, federal policies, and laws.[22] This federal–First Nations interface continued to slowly evolve until 1968, when the National Indian Brotherhood (NIB) materialized as Canada's national Aboriginal organization.[23] An organizing boom followed, and today more than 4,000 organizations and loose First Nations, Inuit, and Métis coalitions have assumed a collection of roles and responsibilities that include providing service delivery and directing economic development initiatives on and off the reserve.[24] The presence of so many Aboriginal organizations did, however, lead federal officials to gradually negotiate more with First Nations leaders (bands and political organizations) seeking augmented self-governing authority.[25]

The key messages that can be drawn from this section are as follows. One, Aboriginal peoples developed contemporary political institutions that reflected the principles of a historic political interface rooted in a nation-to-nation ideal that sought to establish relationships with the newcomers, thus securing their political, social, and economic hegemony. Two, the post-Confederation political institutions were incredibly adaptable and employed an assortment of strategies to challenge state hegemony as colonization began to flourish. Notably, the primary organizations all approved of negotiations as a fundamental method while avoiding militant confrontations. Finally, contemporary Aboriginal political actions remain informed by the historical belief in the importance of negotiations that encourage the use of multiple strategies to protect (in this case) economic development plans.[26] As will be further elaborated on, the ability of First Nations to adapt to various political contexts remains a potent strategy into the contemporary period. The following sections examine specific strategies employed by First Nations seeking to establish provincial First Nations gaming industries.

Aboriginal Rights Challenges

In 1981, the Shawanaga First Nation in Ontario established the Shawanaga First Nation lottery law and the Shawanaga First Nation lottery authority, the latter being vested with the authority to select its members.[27] It is evident from these actions that the First Nation officials believed their unique status as self-governing agents granted them the authority to operate a gaming house. Gaming operations commenced, and band councilors pronounced Shawanaga an independent nation with the inherent right to self-government. Acting on their assertion as a self-governing jurisdiction, the Shawanaga First Nation Council passed two resolutions in August 1987, which, according to its reading of section 81 of the Indian Act, authorized the council to pass local gaming bylaws. Further, the council members remained steadfast in their claims that reserve gaming operations were shielded from provincial laws by virtue of Section 91(24) of the British North America Act of 1867, which recognizes Canada's exclusive responsibility for "Indians, and Lands reserved for the Indians." Later that year the Ontario Provincial Police (OPP) filed charges against Shawanaga chief Roger Jones for operating an illegal gaming house.[28]

Several Canadian First Nations officials followed Shawanaga's lead by proclaiming their interest in launching casinos, and in the early 1980s approached provincial officials to initiate negotiations. First Nation leaders explored American case studies investigating how various cities and towns with casinos and other types of gambling improved their economies vis-à-vis increased government revenues.

First Nations leaders were also intrigued by American Indian efforts at advancing their sovereignty claims by establishing high-stakes bingo operations and, later, reservation casinos. Unlike their Canadian counterparts, however, U.S. tribes have certain powers of jurisdiction within reservation boundaries, including the powers to "determine their respective forms of government (e.g., craft constitutions), define citizenship, pass and enforce laws through their own police forces and courts, collect taxes, regulate the domestic affairs of their citizens, and regulate property use (e.g., through zoning, permitting, environmental regulation, and the like). And like states, American Indian governments have the power to determine whether they will engage in gaming operations."[29] Even so, the U.S. Indian gaming model was the single available source for scrutiny, and First Nations leaders, in many cases, studied it closely.

First Nations interested in reserve casinos began proclaiming an inherent right to control reserve gaming. Reflecting the Federation of Saskatchewan Indians (FSI) conclusions of the late 1970s, "We have never surrendered" sovereignty, which is a both an "inherent and absolute" right.[30] FSI representatives further argued that First Nations governments traditionally exercised the powers of sovereign nations, the most fundamental being the right to govern their people and territory under their own laws and customs.[31] "Inherent" in this case meant that neither Canada's Parliament nor any foreign government branch had the authority to grant the right of self-government. It also meant that First Nations possessed that right of self-governance, a principle confirmed by the treaty process and by the treaties themselves.[32] There were, in effect, two avenues to achieving recognition of these rights. One involved petitioning the courts for a determination of claim. The other was to utilize more forceful tactics to compel its recognition, which Manitoba and Saskatchewan First Nations pursued.

In late 1992, Manitoba's Roseau River Indian Band chief Lawrence Henry announced his plans to open a twenty-four-hour casino with 350 slot machines. The goal was to financially infuse his community with much-needed revenue and the jobs needed to help mitigate the negative impacts of a 75 percent unemployment rate.[33] Citing an Aboriginal right to control reserve gambling, Roseau River business-man and future chief Terry Nelson stated, "We view ourselves as sovereign. We have never assumed the Canadian Criminal Code [or] . . . Constitution," while adding, "There is no Canadian court that will decide . . . sovereign rights at Roseau."[34] By January 1993, the community had expanded its slot machine and bingo operations by bringing in blackjack tables and additional slot machines.[35] Responding to this overt challenge to provincial jurisdiction, the Manitoba justice minister, Jim McCrae, informed the media, "The law is there for all of us. We can't have different laws for different groups in this country." He also warned that he would shut down any band attempt to add to the thirty illegal slot machines operating in the community meeting hall backroom, and that the Royal Canadian Mounted Police (RCMP) would be asked "to carry out their responsibilities" by closing the casino.[36] Manitoba's First Nations leaders responded by reasserting their sovereignty and creating a parallel Indian gaming commission. As expected, the Manitoba government denied First Nations sovereignty existed and, accordingly, refused to acknowledge the First Nations gaming authority.[37]

The key points of First Nations' contention were the province's failure to acknowledge what their leaders claimed to be their inherent right to control reserve gaming, and Manitoba officials' unwillingness to consider integrating First Nations into the growing provincial gaming industry (slot machines had recently been placed in hundreds of rural hotels, and rigorous debates had begun among various local legion hall and community club operators demanding access to electronic gambling). Several First Nations leaders and band members were resolved to improve their economic prospects "by whatever means necessary." According to Nelson, "Roseau River is dangerous to the Canadian and Manitoba governments because they know what's at stake," while adding that, despite provincial warnings to the contrary, "We're going to do it anyway. Our people are not armed, but we are going to be very public about our right to defend ourselves." Roseau River band councilor Ed Hayden helped clarify the issue: Manitoba officials were concerned about losing gambling revenue to First Nations, a claim that Manitoba assistant deputy attorney general Stu Whitley countered by reminding all involved of the recently negotiated bilateral gaming agreements between the province and several bands, including Roseau River, which permitted on-reserve bingo and break-open-ticket games. Whitley further indicated that First Nations threats aside, it was not possible to expand provincial gambling operations by adding First Nations controlled video slot machines. The situation worsened after Roseau River's leadership publicly threatened to launch casinos, which compelled Whitley to issue his strongest warning to date: "There are other options [as opposed to confrontation] at our disposal. We have a plan. It will not involve putting people at risk."[38] On January 19, 1993, the RCMP entered the Roseau River, Fort Alexander, Waterhen, Pine Creek, and Sandy Bay First Nations and seized four-dozen video slot machines and other gaming equipment, such as bingo cards and break-open lottery tickets.[39]

Soon after the Manitoba RCMP raid, White Bear First Nation chief Bernie Shepherd, along with Brian Standingready and several other band councilors, announced their intention to build a casino. Located in Saskatchewan's southeast corner, White Bear had a registered population of just over 2,000 and limited development potential. Concerned with the declaration, provincial officials contacted Shepherd to inform him that responsibility for all gaming activities, including reserve casinos, was vested with the province. Since no indication as to whether the province would negotiate was forthcoming, Shepherd proceeded to cobble together a loose collection of American partners and opened a casino inside White Bear's golf clubhouse on February 26, 1993.[40] Anticipating provincial opposition, Shepherd informed the media and provincial officials prior to its opening that the White Bear people were claiming an inherent right to operate the casino. Shepherd also stated that since the operation was located on reserve land (federal Crown land), his and White Bear First Nations' actions were shielded from provincial jurisdiction. The band council noted for those concerned that they had obtained the necessary business experience by visiting U.S. tribal casinos. Similar to the Manitoba context, Saskatchewan officials replied that the casino was an illegal gaming house according to the *Criminal Code (Canada)*.[41]

Provincial officials were then informed that Shepherd would voluntarily shut down the casino and petition the provincial court for a determination of the casino's status.[42] Premier Roy Romanow ignored the proposal and on March 22, 1993, mobilized the RCMP to conduct a 4:00 a.m. raid on the White Bear casino. A thirty-six-member tactical team armed with assault rifles and surveillance helicopter support seized 115 slot machines, six card tables, financial records, and between $70,000 and $125,000 cash.[43] The casino maintenance crew, security personnel, and a handful of employees tabulating the evening's receipts were arrested, and charges were filed against Shepherd; Standingready; Alan King, the band's U.S. consulting partner; and King's business partner, Susan Alsteen.[44] The casino's closure generated public sympathy for the White Bear people, and when the trial commenced later that fall, the judge ruled that Shepherd and his associates truly believed that the White Bear First Nation had the jurisdiction to regulate gaming on its lands and did not have the guilty intent required for the trial to proceed. All charges were dismissed.[45]

Reflecting on the two confrontations thus asserting the Aboriginal right to control reserve gambling, the Roseau River and White Bear First Nations took a page from the Shawanaga First Nation playbook and asserted their Aboriginal right to control local economic development by establishing casinos as a self-determining act. In each instance, provincial officials responded by mobilizing the RCMP to shut down what were publicly described as illegal operations. One must remain cognizant that federal officials were unsure of what Aboriginal rights were in relation to First Nations gaming, and chose a deliberate approach to assessing First Nations claims. Perhaps that is why Roseau River and White Bear leaders chose to act unilaterally, without provincial approval. It was apparent that by asserting Aboriginal rights, the First Nations were signaling their equal political standing and that Canada—not the provinces—had formal responsibility for Indian affairs, and to negotiate with First Nations. One must also consider that the 1980s were the most significant political period for First Nations peoples since Confederation. First Nations' lobbying efforts resulted in the federal government initiating the Penner Report, recognizing Aboriginal self-government; the inclusion of section 37 in the Constitution Act, mandating the First Ministers Conferences between 1983 and 1987 to define Aboriginal self-government; the Ministerial Task Force on Program Review (the Nielsen Report) in 1986; and the Indian Self-Government Community Negotiations policy statement of 1986.[46] These developments were considered a means of partially reversing "hundreds of years of oppressive government policies and neglect, and to improve their intolerable socio-economic condition," which empowered First Nations to respond to actual and perceived injustices.[47]

These two confrontations over First Nations gaming also occurred on the heels of the Oka confrontation in Quebec. At the heart of what was dubbed the "Indian Summer" of 1990, the seventy-nine-day crisis (the product of a centuries-long land dispute) occupied the Kahnawake and Kanesatake communities, the Quebec provincial government, and Oka Township. Following an exchange of gunfire between the occupiers and the Surete du Quebec (Quebec Provincial Police) that left one officer dead, Ottawa mobilized the Canadian forces to aid the civil authorities—a decision that ensured the dispute remained front-page news for its duration.[48] When the smoke settled, Prime Minister Brian Mulroney was faced with the prospect of negotiating with what many in the media dubbed "Indian" terrorists. Anticipating future blockades and occupations, Mulroney opted to establish a $350 million Royal Commission on Aboriginal Peoples (1991–1996) to contextualize the historic and contemporary Aboriginal-Canada relationship and to produce recommendations structured to improve this relationship and defuse the potential for further violence. Oka captured the Canadian public's attention—and, evidently, that of the Roseau River and White Bear leadership—and remains for many *the* symbol of Aboriginal resistance through direct action, which Aboriginal people continue to employ as a caution to neighboring non-Native peoples of the consequences associated with ignoring their demands.[49]

The outcomes of the two minor confrontations in Manitoba and Saskatchewan were mixed. In one sense, First Nations were deemed by the public to be little more than aggressive nationalists unwilling to pursue justice according to recognized channels, and who consciously espoused a confrontational rhetoric that did not bode well for hopeful entrepreneurs reliant on non-Aboriginal revenues for success. As Belanger and Lackenbauer have shown, confronting governments in such a fashion does little more than establish an adversarial relationship while alienating community members and federal and provincial politicians, all the while producing limited results.[50] Yet the confrontations also signaled the length that First Nations were prepared to go to in order to establish localized economic development. Soon thereafter the Saskatchewan and Ontario New Democratic Party (NDP)[51] premiers both responded by advocating negotiations as the means of resolving their respective disputes with First Nations seeking reserve casinos. Manitoba officials (and those watching closely in Alberta) were slower to respond, but, eventually, they also agreed to negotiate with First Nations, albeit several years later. After this first stage, however, First Nations casino aspirations were clouded by the threat of violence, which in turn demanded First Nations modify their public persona if they were to be successful in their negotiations with provincial officials who refused to be seen negotiating at the end of a gun barrel. Interestingly, First Nations and provincial politicians initiated informal meetings that proceeded slowly, due primarily to the fact that the Canadian courts were evaluating an Aboriginal self-governing right to control reserve gambling claims.

Aboriginal Rights Claims

As the Roseau River and White Bear events were unfolding, court proceedings were under way in Ontario to clarify the Aboriginal right to control gaming. The lack of success in compelling the Saskatchewan and Manitoba provincial governments to allow the construction of reserve casinos suggested to many that a new strategy was required. In Ontario, Shawanaga once again set the tone that all First Nations interested in reserve casinos closely scrutinized: they sought to have their Aboriginal right to control reserve casinos recognized. Community leaders reasoned that if court proceedings were initiated, they could cite the Indian Act in support of its claim to jurisdiction over reserve gaming. To challenge provincial jurisdiction, Shawanaga leaders contended that section 81 of the Indian Act provided for band "control and prohibition of public games" and "other amusements," a strategy many First Nations leaders considered formal governmental acknowledgment of the First Nations' right "to control public games," including high-stakes bingos, and ultimately the key to their future prosperity.[52]

Choosing legal recourse through Canada's courts is a considerably complex and time-consuming process. Whereas the outcomes associated with militant activity and confrontations and employing the courts are ostensibly the same—both strategies seek to compel the formal recognition of an Aboriginal right to manage reserve casinos—the tactics differ considerably and inform non-Aboriginal observers in specific ways. Direct action's value had been questioned since the early days of militant Aboriginal activities. While it can quickly raise public awareness, it can also undermine local community stability and produce poor public relations.[53] The courts, on the other hand, were considered a socially accepted mediation tool that could potentially resolve the scope of Aboriginal rights. Most First Nations leaders gravitated to time-consuming negotiations over militant actions due in part to the jurisdictional complexity that Roseau River and White Bear leaders faced. Perhaps as important, an affirmative court decision would clarify whether the proclaimed Aboriginal right to control reserve gaming trumped provincial jurisdiction over reserve gaming.[54]

Prior to the confrontations in Manitoba and Saskatchewan, the Supreme Court of Canada had spoken to the issue of Aboriginal rights in relation to the separation of powers and gambling in *R. v. Furtney*. The accused in this case were charged with counseling licensees of bingo lottery schemes to violate the terms and conditions of their licenses, specifically the so-called 15–20 percent rule, whereby a maximum of 15 percent of the revenues can go to management costs and a minimum of 20 percent must go to the charity. The trial judge found that the *Criminal Code (Canada)* provisions purporting to delegate power to the lieutenant governor in council exceeded the scope of its powers and dismissed the charges. On appeal, however, the Supreme Court concluded that the provinces were simply asserting their constitutional powers according to section 92 of the British North America Act (1867).[55] The *Furtney* court held that the federal and the provincial governments both held jurisdiction over gaming. Whereas the federal government prohibited gaming generally, it permitted exceptions through the delegation of administrative responsibility for gaming to the province. *Furtney* stands for the proposition that a provincial legislature has jurisdiction to enact laws in the gaming area subject only to Parliament's paramountcy in the case of a clash between federal and provincial legislation.[56] Notably, a provincial legislature's jurisdiction in this area is limited, and, according to the court, the province cannot prohibit and punish in the interest of public morality, because such legislation is criminal law.[57] In a related case, and one that undermined the Shawanaga (and all First Nations interested in reserve casinos) legal position, the Alberta provincial court ruled in *E. v. Gladue and Kirby*[58] that the Indian Act did not supersede "the application of the criminal code to gambling on a reserve."[59]

Although the self-governing Aboriginal right to control reserve gaming had not as yet been determined, this would change after the OPP charged Chief Howard Pamajewon and former chief Howard Jones with running an unlawful gaming house later in 1987, and charged Eagle Lake chief Arnold Gardner and band members Allan Gardner and Jack Pitchenese with running a bingo operation without a provincial gaming license on November 3, 1990. Similar to their Saskatchewan and Manitoba counterparts, the Eagle Lake and Shawanaga band councils challenged the provincial belief in their right to control First Nations gaming and opened an illegal operation that the police subsequently shut down. Unlike their counterparts, they decided to pursue recognition of their Aboriginal rights to control reserve gaming in court. Interestingly enough, the Ontario Lotteries Corporation (OLC) had offered the Shawanaga band a license to conduct gaming operations. Shawanaga representatives politely declined the offer, claiming that the establishment of any reserve economic initiative was an inherent right of a self-governing nation.[60] To accept a license from a provincial agency would compromise the Shawanaga First Nation's political authority. The struggle now turned toward establishing that First Nations had an inherent right to conduct reserve gaming enterprises. Shawanaga chief Roger Jones vigorously trumpeted the Aboriginal right to self-government. "We regard ourselves as a sovereign nation," he said. "We sign treaties and we have the right to pass laws in our lands and if we wish to pass a law that's going to generate revenue for our community in whatever manner we see fit, we have the right to do that."[61] Jones further addressed the concept of sovereignty and self-government before the Royal Commission on Aboriginal Peoples in 1993: "Sovereignty is difficult to define because it is intangible, it cannot be seen or touched. It is very much inherent, an awesome power, a strong feeling or the belief of a people. What can be seen, however, is the exercise of Aboriginal powers."[62]

Jones and Pamajewon were convicted in March 1993 of keeping a common gaming house contrary to section 201(1) of the *Criminal Code (Canada)*.[63] Seeking an appeal, Shawanaga legal counsel David Nahwegahbow indicated that he would pursue the case to the Supreme Court, because, in his mind, the issue was a constitutional question dealing with whether or not the provinces had the right to regulate First Nations' interests.[64] Supreme Court of Canada justice William Stevenson countered Nahwegahbow in his response, indicating "such a mistaken belief was no answer to the charges since ignorance of the law is no defense to breaking it."[65] Stevenson noted that the band did not challenge the validity of the *Criminal Code (Canada)* gaming section, although it did request that the court not make any statements that may adversely affect legal issues concerning Aboriginal self-government.[66]

In 1996, the Supreme Court in *Pamajewon* determined that the Shawanaga and Eagle Lake First Nations in Ontario did not possess the Aboriginal right to control and regulate reserve casino gaming. The court determined that the litigants failed to demonstrate gaming's centrality to Ojibwa culture or its practice as connected to "the self-identity and self-preservation of the aboriginal societies involved here."[67] Concluding that gaming was not an Aboriginal right, the Supreme Court determined that on-reserve gambling facilities were not exempt from provincial legislation regulating gaming. Although the possibility of recognizing Aboriginal rights in another case has not been exhausted, the original claim that gaming was an inherent Aboriginal right was answered for the Shawanaga and Eagle Lake First Nations. The case was related to self-government as an Aboriginal right, and not exclusively to self-government as an exercise of Aboriginal title.[68] The litigants asserted a broad right of self-government, and they claimed that this right includes the authority to regulate gaming activities on the reserve, an argument the court declined to consider. Instead, it deferred to the lower court of appeal that indicated "there is no evidence that gambling on the reserve lands generally was ever the subject matter of aboriginal regulation. Moreover, there is no evidence of an historic involvement in anything resembling the high stake gambling in issue in these cases."[69]

The *Pamajewon* court was critical of the litigant's claim, citing it as too general, while concluding that, for an activity to be recognized an Aboriginal right, it must be "related to a particular custom, practice, tradition or activity."[70] The *Van Der Peet* (1996) court's conclusion that the activities in question must be present in the period prior to European contact informed the court's analysis.[71] Aboriginal rights were consequently characterized as historical rights informed by the attendant customs and practices at the time of contact with Europeans that had a limited ability to evolve; their postcontact evolution cannot be acknowledged as an Aboriginal right. Finally, should historical exercise in any way become disengaged from contemporary practice, historic continuity and tradition are shattered, and the Aboriginal right is considered nonexistent. This test has been widely criticized and is subtly being restructured, even if it remains the metric guiding justices when determining Aboriginal rights claims.

To summarize, politicians, the media, and the general public were more accepting of First Nations legal claims, for they better reflected what was deemed to be an acceptable avenue of dispute resolution. The conflict regarding the efficacy of reserve casinos had not ebbed, and many believed a legal opinion would help resolve confounding questions about the notion of Aboriginal rights and self-government's meaning, both of which continue to evolve. It is important to note that White Bear and Roseau River leaders never publicly announced their intent to pursue their rights in the courts. Rather, it was Ontario's Shawanaga First Nation who had initiated the case that would decide against the self-governing right to control reserve gaming. By the mid-1990s, negotiations in Ontario, Saskatchewan, and Alberta (newly entered into the discussion) appeared to be leading to the creation of formal provincial First Nations gaming policies and reserve casino construction.

Negotiations

On the surface it appeared as though the Roseau River and White Bear confrontations failed. However, not long after each event provincial officials announced their willingness to consider and eventually agree to negotiations that would lead to reserve casinos acceptance. Interestingly, as discussed above, despite the Supreme Court's decision that the provinces held the right to control high-stakes gambling in reserve communities, thus compelling First Nations to negotiate for that very privilege, consultation had been ongoing in Ontario since 1992 and in Saskatchewan since 1993, while initial discussions in Alberta dated to 1993.[72] First Nations leaders remained steadfast in their claims that reserve gaming operations were shielded from provincial laws, and that First Nations had an Aboriginal right to control reserve gaming. As the Roseau River and White Bear confrontations demonstrated, overtly challenging the state was unproductive, but so too was the Ontario approach of engaging in time-consuming and expensive legal battles. Arguably, these events helped push negotiations along in provinces that had at least been mulling over the issue of reserve gaming. Accordingly, once negotiations began, sui generis policy environments and on the ground gambling industries emerged, demonstrating similarities and differences. The following discussion elaborates these dynamics while establishing the key policy markers guiding the evolution of First Nations gaming in each province, and, ultimately, the concessions demanded of First Nations during the negotiations.

Ontario

In 1992, in response to discussion with Ontario First Nations leaders, Premier Bob Rae announced his intention to open a reserve casino. By February 1994, fourteen provincial First Nations had their sights set on hosting the casino that would, according to provincial officials, distribute profits to the province's First Nations through a First Nations fund. Premier Rae announced on December 5, 1994, that the Mnjikaning First Nation had been selected as the site. Casino Rama would be situated on First Nations land, the Mnjikaning reserve, and would be run by an established corporation during its first ten years of operations. A request for proposals stipulated that the operator's costs prior to construction would include the construction of a recreational facility and a seniors' home, and the establishment of a trust fund to develop a gambling addictions program. The Mnjikaning proposal was considered the most attractive for a number of reasons, the most important being the revenue-sharing formula, which would see 65 percent of net revenues divided among the province's 133 First Nations. The remaining 35 percent would remain with the Mnjikaning First Nation to deal with increased traffic's impact on reserve infrastructure and to ensure programs for problem gaming in the community were funded. Following the announced opening date, the Progressive Conservatives (PC)[73] defeated the NDP and immediately imposed a 20 percent Win Tax on Casino Rama gross revenues.

Saskatchewan

In 1993, the FSIN approached Premier Roy Romanow (NDP) to discuss reserve casino construction.[74] From the premier's perspective, the FSIN's inability to speak on behalf of many of the province's First Nations, tribal councils, and individual band councils rendered the organization less than effective. Negotiations nevertheless proceeded, and two years after the White Bear raid, the Gaming Framework Agreement (GFA) and the Casino Operating Agreement (COA) were implemented in 1995. At the GFA's center was the revenue-sharing formula, including a set of guidelines delineating how the revenues were to be spent by recipient First Nations. Specifically, the provincial government would receive 37.5 percent of net revenues, 37.5 percent would go to the First Nations Trust, and the residual 25 percent would be allocated to four provincial Community Development Corporations (CDCs). Each CDC was established to aid in distributing one-quarter of the net profit share pursuant to the Framework Agreement in an effort to stimulate First Nations economic development; fund reserve justice and health initiatives; finance reserve education and cultural development; improve community infrastructure; and develop senior and youth programs and other charitable purposes. Each CDC was recognized as a corporate body with a board of directors.[75] The Saskatchewan government, in 2007, lowered its share of First Nations gaming revenues from 37.5 percent to 25 percent while raising the overall First Nations share of profits to 75 percent. The revised revenue-sharing agreement has led to improved First Nations development, which is directly attributable to an infusion of gaming revenues. As of 2016–2017, SIGA is successfully operating six casinos.

Alberta

In 1993, the Tsuu T'ina First Nation (southwest of Calgary) and the Enoch Cree First Nation (west of Edmonton) were awarded licenses to hold super-bingos that guaranteed jackpots exceeding $10,000. That year, the Tsuu T'ina turned a $100,000 profit, which led to immediate calls from provincial First Nations leaders to create an independent First Nations Gaming Commission.[76] First Nations leaders advocated for a policy model ensuring all bands would benefit equally from any reserve casino developments. As early as 1996, a plan was placed on the agenda that would have allocated 10 percent of First Nation casino profits to a fund benefiting the province's First Nations, while the First Nation, or the management company running the casino, would receive 50 percent of the profits. Alberta's licensed charities would receive the remaining 40 percent.[77] First Nations balked at the proposal and remained noncommittal while persevering with their lobby efforts. In September 2000, Premier Klein (PC) proposed a new policy that would allocate all reserve casino profits to the provincial First Nations, and in December he went public with his support, thus offering First Nations leaders an important

TABLE. Key Provisions of Each Provincial First Nations Casino Policy

	ONTARIO	SASKATCHEWAN	ALBERTA
Outside Casino Operator Required	●		●
Revenue Sharing Agreement	●	●	●
Provincial Fee from Casino Revenues	●	●	●
Casinos Licensed as Charities			●
Prescribed Use of Casino Revenues	●	●	●
Problem Gambling Assistance Fund	●		
Ad Hoc Approach	●	●	●

Source: Yale D. Belanger, "Are Canadian First Nations Casinos Providing Maximum Benefits? Appraising Canada's First Nations Casino Industry in Ontario, Saskatchewan, and Alberta, 1996–2010," *UNLV Gaming Research and Review* 18, no. 2 (2014): 65–84.

vote of confidence. First Nations were pleased with the premier's pronouncements, and, one month later, on January 21, 2001, the First Nations Gaming Policy (FNGP) was ratified. It did contain one unanticipated modification: a proviso directing 30 percent of all First Nations casinos' slot machine revenues to the Alberta Lottery Fund for provincial charitable use.[78] Without publicly acknowledging the 30 percent proviso's inclusion, the FNGP, provincial officials claimed, would afford First Nations the opportunity "to support economic, social and community development projects as well as use charitable gaming proceeds for initiatives such as infrastructure and life skills training."[79]

As the "Key Provisions of Each Provincial First Nations Casino Policy" table demonstrates, each gaming province initially favored First Nation leaders' desires for economic independence, despite a government inability or unwillingness to consider First Nation casino applicants as analogous to non-Aboriginal casino operators.[80] Each province has *Criminal Code (Canada)*–granted jurisdiction over gaming, and each has developed, in conjunction with First Nations, distinct provincial First Nations gaming policies. The provinces of Ontario, Saskatchewan, and Alberta have exploited the *Criminal Code (Canada)* authority by demanding concessions and thus prescribing negotiated outcomes, much to the annoyance of First Nations battling for recognition of their inherent Aboriginal right to control reserve gaming. As the table also illustrates, Ontario may have had a sense of how to pursue a First Nations gaming policy, but in the end, all provinces responded to First Nations' requests to operate reserve casinos in an ad hoc fashion, leading to a less structured organic process. From a provincial perspective, reserve casinos were never seen as products of, nor did they represent elements of, Aboriginal self-government, and Alberta demanded that the host First Nations abdicate self-governing authority by licensing their casino operations as charities.[81] In sum, the provinces leveraged their *Criminal Code (Canada)*–assigned authority to approve casino licenses and fashion First Nations gaming policies reflecting provincial desires. Certain provisions permitted each province to dictate through internal oversight policies how First Nations could spend their revenues as well as the guidelines to releasing the provincially held casino revenues. Alberta and Ontario demanded outside casino operators be brought in, whereas Saskatchewan permitted the FSIN to establish SIGA for those purposes.

As the above discussion also illustrates, despite being negotiated independently of one another, the provincial policies, when compared, are ideologically similar: they were established to ensure provincial oversight over First Nations casino operations, spending, and provincial development through imposed contributions to provincial coffers. These actions guaranteed that the provinces retained centralized authority for regulating First Nations casino operations while simultaneously restricting First Nations economic and political agency. Each provincial approach innovatively enabled the provincial gaming bureaucracy's expansion during a period of economic reforms by assigning to First Nations annual fees for the privilege of operating casinos. However, no provisions were included in Alberta or Ontario to ensure portions of overall revenues were directed toward establishing responsive treatment programs, and the funding Saskatchewan demanded be set aside is minimal at best.

Discussion

As noted earlier, academics tend to train their investigative lenses on the socioeconomic and political ramifications of First Nations casinos. Frequently overlooked in this environment is the response to extracommunity forces that influenced how First Nations leaders bargained their casinos into existence. Canadians and, by extension, their elected representatives initially framed First Nations casinos as contested sites of immorality that, even upon reaching financial success, would lead to community ruination. First Nations found that they were forced to set the record straight by forging public personas and adopting specific strategies to secure what they claimed to be an inherent right to manage reserve gaming. Adding to this intricacy was a history of Canadian Indian policy and national economic development processes that failed to recognize First Nations as significant players, which, as Tough noted, marginalized Aboriginal peoples to a degree that they arguably remain stranded on Canada's economic periphery. In this setting, First Nations responded by establishing unique strategies that reflected the principles of historic political interface.

At the outset First Nations in Ontario, Manitoba, and Saskatchewan opened gaming establishments without provincial permission that the police eventually shut down. While First Nations in each province, including Alberta, proclaimed a historic Aboriginal right to control local economic development, Manitoba and Saskatchewan First Nations adopted an assertive stance that involved (subtly) threatening physical resistance in the wake of the RCMP's entry into reserve communities. The latter strategy, reliant on violence or the threat of violence, is one that First Nations organizations tended to avoid in lieu of negotiations. Saskatchewan, Manitoba, and Ontario First Nations were all charged with criminal offenses for operating illegal gaming establishments. It was the Ontario First Nations that decided to pursue a legal determination of their rights. Though they had never challenged the provincial government in a similar fashion the threat of violence (real or perceived) hung in the air, as Oka was still fresh in everyone's minds.[82] Rather than be seen as potentially militant First Nations working outside provincial jurisdiction, they evolved into litigants working within accepted legal norms, an important moment that garnered Ontario officials' goodwill. Why Manitoba and Saskatchewan First Nations chose militant tactics is not fully understood, especially considering that the Shawanaga case was, by that point, working its way to the Supreme Court. Given the snail's pace and extreme costs associated with litigating complex claims, adopting militant tactics validates legal scholar Bradford Morse's conclusion that extrajudicial remedies—such as direct action tactics—are often-times considered the only viable options for Aboriginal peoples seeking change.[83] Or, at a time when Oka still loomed large, perhaps Saskatchewan and Manitoba leaders believed they could leverage a militant public image to induce provincial accession to their demands.

The timing was, however, inopportune and did little more than illustrate to the public and politicians alike the politically unstable nature of reserve casinos, thus confirming what many already believed: volatile First Nations governments were not suited to operate reserve casinos successfully. Yet by early 1993, officials in

Alberta, Saskatchewan, and Ontario had agreed to discuss what would eventually morph into formal negotiations leading to the construction of a small gaming industry of reserve casinos located in those three provinces. Reflecting on Tough's argument, however, it is striking how closely these negotiations duplicated past colonial relationships, which were characterized by First Nations' subordination to a colonial power, and how, yet again, officials outside the communities were determining from afar what appropriate local economic development strategies should look like. This is not a trivial issue when one considers that the First Nations involved "sought an equitable political and financial arrangement as they pursued improved living conditions that had been negatively impacted by previous federal and provincial colonial policies. Simply put, embedded colonial norms compelled First Nations acquiescence on several levels during and following negotiations."[84]

The mixture of failed direct action and an unfavorable court decision ironically may have secured First Nations a seat at the negotiating table, but it also left them at the mercy of provincial officials seeking to maintain jurisdictional supremacy over reserve gaming. The federal government's refusal to negotiate and the provincial officials' refusal to compromise their authority over gambling-related concerns arguably left First Nations leaders with little choice in the matter. All the same, negotiations in Ontario and Saskatchewan were quickly concluded, followed by Manitoba in the late 1990s and Alberta in the early 2000s. It is evident from the negotiations that provincial officials were intent on retaining a significant level of jurisdictional authority, which influenced the respective policies' outcomes.[85] In particular all of the provinces discussed in this chapter leveraged their *Criminal Code (Canada)*–assigned authority to approve casino licenses while enabling officials to fashion First Nations gaming policies with limited First Nations input. The provinces crafted internally favorable policies that provided First Nations a taste of financial success, but that did not lead to the anticipated financial transformation reserve casinos initially promised. These actions guaranteed that each province retained the centralized authority to regulate First Nation casino operations while also restricting First Nations economic and political agency. It once again appears as though First Nations and mainstream Canada in many ways remain on separate economic trajectories, institutionalized through policy that Aboriginal political organizations and First Nations councils continue to challenge, as reserve economies attempt to subsist from the margins.

Final Thoughts

In the span of a few years, First Nations emerged from economic purgatory to seek new gambling-related opportunities only to be identified as unworthy in one sense (when they sought to work on their own outside of provincial jurisdiction), as militants claiming an inherent right to control local development in another, and as litigants seeking recognition of their Aboriginal rights through accepted legal channels in another. Unfortunately, many fell prey to provincial opportunism that ultimately compelled First Nations leaders to concede political and economic agency for the privilege of running reserve casinos. In fact, each province evaluated in this chapter developed gaming policies that included a key provision diverting substantial gaming revenues away from struggling First Nations communities and into their own treasuries, thereby fueling their own development through economic exploitation.[86] Yet little effort to date has been directed at exploring the unique political and economic environments from which these images emerged or, more importantly how First Nations specifically countered their social and political impacts.[87] While none of the approaches discussed earlier was on its own successful, I would suggest that resistance and litigation needed to unfold if provincial officials were to be convinced of the need to engage with First Nations leadership. This chapter hopefully has provided some clarity and the basis from which additional work can be developed.

NOTES

1. The term "First Nation" is used here to denote a reserve community, or band. The phrase "Aboriginal people" indicates any one of the three legally defined culture groups that form what is known as Aboriginal Peoples in Canada (Métis, Inuit, and Indian) and who self-identify as such. The term "Indian," as used in legislation or policy, will also appear in discussions concerning such legislation or policy. The term "Indigenous" here does not represent a legal category. Rather, it is used to describe the descendants of groups in a territory at the time when other groups of different cultures or ethnic origin arrived there, groups that have almost preserved intact the customs and traditions of their ancestors similar to those characterized as Indigenous, and those that have been placed under a state structure that incorporates national, social, and cultural characteristics distinct from their own.

2. Yale D. Belanger, "The Saskatchewan Indian Gaming Authority's Approach to Securing

Public Trust, 2000–2004," *Journal of Aboriginal Economic Development* 7, no. 1 (2010): 66–80.

3. Yale D. Belanger, "Are Canadian First Nations Casinos Providing Maximum Benefits? Appraising Canada's First Nations Casino Industry in Ontario, Saskatchewan, and Alberta, 1996–2010," *UNLV Gaming Research and Review* 18, no. 2 (2014): 65–84.

4. Yale D. Belanger, *Gambling with the Future: The Evolution of Aboriginal Gaming in Canada* (Saskatoon: Purich Publishing, 2006).

5. For this argument, see Frank Tough, "From the 'Original Affluent Society' to the 'Unjust Society,'" *Journal of Aboriginal Economic Development* 4, no. 2 (2005): 26–65.

6. Ibid., 50.

7. Ibid., 51.

8. The government of Canada's new Framework for Aboriginal Economic Development (Minister of Indian Affairs and Northern Development, 2009) identifies specifically four strategic priorities, the first being "strengthening Aboriginal entrepreneurship." The purpose of this framework is to promote economic development through new business formation and improved employment opportunities for Aboriginal peoples. At present, Aboriginal peoples fall far behind non-Aboriginal peoples in Canada on employment, unemployment, and participation rates, and unfortunately this bleak situation worsened in the economic downturn (Statistics Canada, 2011).

9. James Tully, *Strange Multiplicity: Constitutionalism in an Age of Diversity* (New York: Cambridge University Press, 1995), 23.

10. Canada, *For Seven Generations: An Information Legacy of the Royal Commission on Aboriginal Peoples* (Ottawa: Canada Communications Group, 1996).

11. Immanuel Kant, *The Metaphysics of Morals* (Cambridge: Cambridge University Press, 1991), 43, 121.

12. Jeremy Waldron, "Cultural Identity and Civic Responsibility," in *Citizenship in Diverse Societies*, ed. Will Kymlicka and Wayne Norman (Don Mills: Oxford University Press, 2000), 155.

13. Michael Ignatieff, *The Rights Revolution* (Toronto: House of Anansi Press, 2000), 86–87.

14. Tough, "From the 'Original Affluent Society.'"

15. Canada, *For Seven Generations*, 1996.

16. See J. R. Miller, *Compact, Contract, Covenant: Aboriginal Treaty-Making in Canada* (Toronto: University of Toronto Press, 2009); and James (Sa'ke'j) Youngblood Henderson, *Treaty Rights in the Constitution of Canada* (Toronto: Thomson Canada, 2007).

17. RCAP, *For Seven Generations*.

18. Tough, "From the 'Original Affluent Society.'"

19. John S. Milloy, "The Era of Civilization: British Policy for the Indians of Canada, 1830–1860" (PhD diss., Oxford University, 1978).

20. See Sydney Harring, *White Man's Law: Native People in Nineteenth-Century Canadian Jurisprudence* (Toronto: Osgoode Society for Canadian Legal History, 1998). In 1867, the *Connelly v. Woolrich* decision informed First Nations that the sources of law and authority were more diverse than Canadian officials let on, while simultaneously embracing "the right of Aboriginal peoples to conduct their affairs under their own laws, within a larger constitutional framework linking them with the Crown." In this instance a Cree man named John Connolly petitioned the court to determine his claim to a share of his father's estate that was being withheld. The Quebec Superior Court held that the Cree marriage between the two was valid and that the eldest son was entitled to his rightful share of the estate. This decision "portrays Aboriginal peoples as autonomous nations living within the protection of the Crown but retaining their territorial rights, political organizations and common laws." Justice Monk concluded that he had no hesitation in holding that "the Indian political and territorial right, laws, and usages remained in full force" in the Northwest at the relevant time.

21. Yale D. Belanger, "Seeking a Seat at the Table: A Brief History of Indian Political Organizing in Canada, 1870–1951" (PhD diss., Trent University, 2006).

22. For a discussion of the SJC's impact, see Peter Kulchyski, "Anthropology in the Service of the State: Diamond Jenness and Canadian Indian Policy," *Journal of Canadian Studies* 28. no. 2 (1993): 21–50; John Leslie, "Assimilation, Integration, or Termination? The Development of Canadian Indian Policy, 1943–1963" (PhD diss., Carleton University, 1999); and Hugh Shewell, *"Enough to Keep Them Alive": Indian Welfare in Canada, 1873–1965* (Toronto: University of Toronto Press, 2004).

23. See Peter McFarlane, *Brotherhood to Nationhood: George Manuel and the Making of the Modern Indian Movement* (Toronto: Between the Lines, 1993); and George Manuel and Michael Posluns, *The Fourth World: An Indian Reality* (Don Mills, Ontario: Collier Macmillan Canada, 1974).

24. Yale D. Belanger, *Ways of Knowing: An Introduction to Native Studies in Canada*, 2nd ed. (Toronto: Nelson Education, 2014), 237.

25. As this chapter was undergoing final revisions, the Canadian government announced funding cuts to Aboriginal organizations nationally, resulting in massive layoffs.

26. Belanger, "Seeking a Seat at the Table"; Ovide Mercredi and Mary Ellen Turpel, *In the Rapids: Navigating the Future of First Nations* (Toronto: Penguin Books, 1994).

27. Belanger, *Gambling with the Future*, 85.

28. On November 3, 1990, the OPP charged Eagle Lake chief Arnold Gardner and band

members Allan Gardner and Jack Pitchenese with running a bingo operation without a provincial gaming license.

29. Leigh Gardner, Joseph P. Kalt, and Katherine A. Spilde, *Cabazon, The Indian Gaming Regulatory Act, and the Socioeconomic Consequences of American Indian Governmental Gaming: A Ten-Year Review* (Cambridge, MA: The Harvard Project on American Indian Economic Development, 2005), iii.

30. Quoted in Yale D. Belanger and David R. Newhouse, "Reconciling Solitudes: A Critical Analysis of the Self-Government Ideal," in *Aboriginal Self-Government in Canada: Current Trends and Issues*, 3rd ed., ed. Yale D. Belanger (Saskatoon: Purich Publishing, 2008), 1–19.

31. Ibid.

32. Ibid.; see also Henderson, *Treaty Rights*.

33. David Roberts, "Band Raises Stakes with Casino Plan: The Roseau River Indians Are Defying Manitoba's Authority by Expanding Gambling," *Globe and Mail*, January 6, 1993, A4.

34. "Natives Defiant," *Calgary Herald*, September 16, 1991, A7.

35. Roberts, "Band Raises Stakes."

36. George Oake, "Manitoba, Alberta Keep Odds in Their Favour," *Toronto Star*, November 16, 1991, A17.

37. David Roberts, "Band Rejects Canadian Laws, Hearing Told Roseau Reserve Will Offer Tax-free Goods, Gambling, Native Businessman Tells Royal Commission," *Globe and Mail*, December 9, 1992, A8.

38. Ibid.

39. "Chiefs Balk at Reforms to Protest Gambling Raids," *Windsor Star*, January 20, 1993, A2.

40. Belanger, *Gambling with the Future*, 107.

41. For this detailed discussion, see ibid., 107–10.

42. "Natives Open a Casino Despite Saskatchewan Government Opposition," *Globe and Mail*, February 27, 1993, A4.

43. Belanger, *Gambling with the Future*, 107.

44. "Natives Open a Casino," A4.

45. Belanger, *Gambling with the Future*, 108.

46. Menno Boldt, *Surviving as Indians: The Challenge of Self-Government* (Toronto: University of Toronto Press, 1993).

47. David Hawkes, *The Search for Accommodation* (Kingston, ON: Institute of Intergovernmental Relations, 1987), 1.

48. See Warren Skea, "The Canadian Newspaper Industry's Portrayal of the Oka Crisis," *Native Studies Review* 9, no. 1 (1994): 15–31; and Geoffrey York and Loreen Pindera, *People of the*

Pines: The Warriors and the Legacy of Oka (Toronto: McArthur, 1991).

49. There is a significant literature base at this stage even if it remains fairly scattered both in terms of its geographic and conceptual scope.

50. See Yale D. Belanger and P. Whitney Lackenbauer, eds., *Blockades or Breakthroughs? Aboriginal People Confront the Canadian State* (Kingston: McGill-Queen's University Press, 2014).

51. The New Democratic Party (NDP) was founded in 1961 out of the merger of the Co-operative Commonwealth Federation (CCF) and the Canadian Labour Congress (CLC), and bills itself and Canada's social democratic party.

52. Hal Pruden, "An Overview of the Gambling Provisions in Canadian Criminal Law and First Nations Gambling," *Journal of Aboriginal Economic Development* 2, no. 2 (2002): 40. The Shawanaga and Eagle Lake First Nations unilaterally decided to design and implement gaming bylaws without provincial consent.

53. See, for example, Christine Blatchford, *Helpless: Caledonia's Nightmare of Fear and Anarchy, and How the Law Failed All of Us* (Toronto: Doubleday Canada, 2010); Laura Devries, *Conflict in Caledonia: Aboriginal Land Rights and the Rule of Law* (Vancouver: University of British Columbia Press, 2011); Sarah King, *Fishing in Contested Waters: Place and Community in Burnt Church/Esgenoopetitj* (Toronto: University of Toronto Press, 2014); Peter Edwards, *One Dead Indian: The Premier, the Police, and the Ipperwash Crisis* (Toronto: Stoddart, 2001); Sandra Lambertus, *Wartime Images, Peacetime Wounds: The Media and the Gustafsen Lake Standoff* (Toronto: University of Toronto Press, 2004); and Anna J. Willow, *Strong Hearts, Native Lands: Anti-Clearcutting Activism at Grassy Narrows First Nation* (Albany: State University of New York Press, 2012).

54. In December 1985, *Criminal Code (Canada)* amendments prepared by the Department of Justice, the Interprovincial Lottery Corporation, and the provinces formally removed federal authority over lottery schemes and pool betting operations. The bill clarified that a province "could conduct a lottery scheme on or through a computer, video device or slot machine, but could not license others to do so." Prior to this bill, there would have been some who believed that a province could, in theory, license others to conduct lottery schemes using these mechanisms. In sum, federal officials had officially transferred jurisdiction for lotteries and other forms of gaming to the provinces and without taking into consideration First Nations' interests.

55. *R. v. Furtney* 3 S.C.R. (1991), 89. See also Paul K. Frits, "Aboriginal Gaming—Law and Policy," in *Aboriginal Issues Today: A Legal and Business Guide*, ed. Stephen B. Smart and Michael Coyle (Vancouver: Self-Counsel Press, 1997), 228–29.

56. *R. v. Furtney*, 91.

57. Ibid.

58. *E. v. Gladue and Kirby* 30 CCC (3d) (1986) (Alta. Prov. Ct.) 308; *R. v. Furtney.*

59. Frits, "Aboriginal Gaming," 229.

60. Belanger, *Gambling with the Future*, 87.

61. Frits, "Aboriginal Gaming," 229.

62. Chief Roger Jones, presentation made before the Royal Commission on Aboriginal Peoples, public consultation process, June 1, 1993, Record 7/142.

63. *Criminal Code of Canada* (Toronto: Canada Law Book, 1996). Accordingly, "every one who keeps a common gaming house or common betting house is guilty of an indictable offence and liable to imprisonment for a term not exceeding two years."

64. "Native Bingo Illegal, Court Rules," *Toronto Star*, September 27, 1991, A12.

65. "Reserve's Unlicensed Bingo Illegal," *Ottawa Citizen*, September 27, 1991, A4.

66. Ibid.

67. *R. v. Pamajewon* S.C.R. (1996), 821, 825.

68. Belanger, *Gambling with the Future.*

69. *R. v. Pamajewon.*

70. Ibid., 826.

71. *R. v. Van der Peet* 2 S.C.R. (1996) 507 (S.C.C.).

72. For the early days of the Alberta and Saskatchewan policy and negotiations context, see Warren Skea, "Time to Deal: A Comparison of the Native Casino Gambling Policy in Alberta and Saskatchewan" (PhD diss., University of Calgary, 1997). For the Ontario experience, see Darrel Manitowabi, "From Fish Weirs to Casino: Negotiating Neoliberalism at Mnjikaning (Ontario)" (PhD diss., University of Toronto, 2007); and Belanger, *Gambling with the Future.*

73. The Progressive Conservative Party of Canada (PC) began as the Conservative Party in 1867, and changed its name to the Progressive Conservative Party in 1942. The party dissolved in 2003 and reemerged in partnership with the Canadian Alliance Party as the Conservative Party of Canada.

74. From 1958–1982 the organization was known as the Federation of Saskatchewan Indians (FSI). From 1982–2016 it was the Federation of Saskatchewan Indian Nations (FSN). In 2016, the name was changed to the Federation of Sovereign Indigenous Nations (FSIN).

75. Cathy Nilson, "The FSIN–Province of Saskatchewan Gaming Partnership: 1995 to 2002" (M.A. thesis, University of Saskatchewan, 2004).

76. Monte Stewart, "Natives Seeking Own Gaming Commission," *Calgary Herald*, August 29, 1993, A4.

77. Robert J. Williams, Yale D. Belanger, and Jennifer N. Arthur, *Gambling in Alberta: History,*

Current Status, and Socioeconomic Impacts (Edmonton: Alberta Gaming and Liquor Commission, 2011).

78. Yale D. Belanger and Robert J. Williams, "Neoliberalism as Colonial Embrace: Evaluating Alberta's Regulation of First Nations Gaming, 1993–2010," *Business & Politics* 13, no. 4 (2012): 1–34.

79. Yale D. Belanger, Robert J. Williams, and Jennifer N. Arthur, "Casinos and Economic Well-Being: Evaluating the Alberta First Nations' Experience," *Journal of Gambling Business and Economics* 5, no. 1 (2011): 23–45.

80. Belanger, *Gambling with the Future*; Manitowabi, "From Fish Weirs to Casino."

81. Yale D. Belanger and Robert J. Williams, "The First Nations Contribution to Alberta's Charitable Gaming Model: Assessing the Impacts," *Canadian Public Policy* 38, no. 4 (2012): 551–72.

82. See, for example, York and Pindera, *People of the Pines*.

83. Bradford W. Morse, "Permafrost Rights: Aboriginal Self-Government and the Supreme Court in *R. v. Pamajewon*," *McGill Law Journal* 42, no. 4 (1997): 1012–32.

84. Yale D. Belanger, "Indigenous Transnationalism and Alberta First Nation Gaming: Political Compromise or Negotiated Economic Advantage," in *Transnational Indians in the North American West*, eds. Clarissa Confer, Andrae Marak, and Laura Tuennerman (College Station: Texas A&M University Press, 2015), 279.

85. See Belanger, *Gambling with the Future* and Belanger, *First Nations Gaming in Canada*.

86. Belanger, "Are Canadian First Nations Casinos Providing Maximum Benefits?"

87. An exception is Julie Pelletier, "Show Me the Money: American Indian Gaming, Secrecy, and Settler Society," (paper presented at Canadian Association for American Studies Conference, Banff, Alberta, 2014).

Casinos, Culture, and Cash

How Gambling Has Affected Minnesota Tribal Nations

Caroline Laurent

Since the early 1980s, the income generated by Indian gaming establishments has poured a new stream of revenue into reservations. This influx of money became particularly visible after the Indian Gaming Regulatory Act (IGRA) of 1988 was enacted and tribes started high-stakes gaming on a larger scale, based on federally legal foundations. This income has permitted tribal governments to expand or create new programs and services for tribal members, improve social services, and strengthen educational and traditional programs. It has also allowed tribal governments to address the use of tribal representation by outsiders and to weigh in on the perception non-Natives can have of Native cultures in general. Many people, however, disagree on whether the overall impact of tribal casinos has been beneficial or disruptive to tribal cultures. Indeed, the effect of casinos on Indian cultures is double-edged. On one hand, casinos, inherently capitalistic ventures, and the monies they generate can be seen as directly going against tribal traditions—which forcefully emphasize the dangers of greed—and as encouraging cultural erosion or cultural dormancy. Conversely, casinos may enable Indigenous Nations to counteract the pervasive effects of assimilation on their cultures, or at least to reduce nontribal influences, which might lead to a greater emphasis on traditional values. Since the introduction of high stakes casino gaming by tribes, many Indian traditionalists have been suspicious of the cultural impact this form of gambling may have on their communities.[1] One critic is Jim Northrup, a prominent Minnesota Ojibwe writer and advocate of traditional values. In 1993, he stated that "gambling begets greed. The tiger [gaming] is making us forget who we are as a people. Gambling is teaching us not to share."[2]

Certain aspects of casino gaming can have negative effects on Indian communities. Addictions to gambling, alcohol, and cigarettes can be exacerbated by going to casinos—although some of them are "dry" places where no alcohol is served. Some opponents to gambling even take this criticism a step further, stating that addiction to gambling encourages domestic violence and abuse.[3] One of the concerns of local communities, and of some tribal members themselves, is that casino revenues can indirectly fund drug use and illegal activities. Although these issues are real and highly problematic, another, more satisfying perspective should be underlined when looking at how the money generated by casinos has significantly helped Native Nations revive their cultures.

Before analyzing this revival, it is essential to assert a specific definition of that critical concept—culture. As it is considered here, culture encompasses all aspects of society, including beliefs and values, material goods, and knowledge that is learned and transmitted across generations.[4] Education, traditions, and language are the most crucial cultural aspects that will be examined here. In her groundbreaking book about Seminole gaming in Florida, anthropologist Jessica Cattelino explains how the "currency of culture" relates to casinos.[5] Indeed, if the impact of Indian gaming is often studied for political and economic purposes, the cultural consequences and changes need to be given more attention in order to understand the profound transformations taking place in Indian Country.

This chapter endeavors to demonstrate the tangible consequences of gaming revenue on reservations in terms of preservation of culture and how it has helped Native peoples redefine their identity according to their own cultural paradigms. The first section focuses on three Ojibwe reservations situated in Minnesota: Mille Lacs, White Earth, and Fond du Lac.[6] These reservations all have their own specific-ities—different demographics, variable successes, and a range of initiatives—but all have been working on their education systems, traditions, and language. The second part of this study considers various Indigenous cultural aspects that have been revitalized, or that have morphed, thanks to casino money in the United States—but more specifically in Minnesota—including the way tribal Nations approach employment laws and their new ability to oppose the appropriation of their names or identifiable cultural traits without their consent for all types of purposes (businesses, sports, celebrations, or arts). This chapter explores the various creative and unexpected ways in which casinos have helped positively influence the revival of Indian cultures. The final section focuses on the role that casinos play in the lives of Indian tribes, to what extent Native peoples identify with tribally owned casinos, and what these places represent for them. The following pages, therefore, provide some examples of casino revenues supporting tribal efforts to preserve and revitalize values and traditions, and strengthening control of their representations, cultural practices, and identities, at times even enabling the reversal of nontribal influences.

The Cultural Impact of Casinos on Three Minnesota Reservations

The Mille Lacs Band of Ojibwe

Located in east-central Minnesota, the Mille Lacs Band of Ojibwe is a federally recognized tribe whose reservation boundaries are acknowledged by the federal government, but, interestingly, not by the county of Mille Lacs surrounding it.[7] According to the Mille Lacs Band's enrollment department, the estimated number of enrolled Band members in the year 1990 was just under 1,900. After the two Mille Lacs casinos opened in 1991 and 1992, the total number of enrolled Band members more than doubled. This population surge occurred partly because a number of individuals whose ancestors belonged to the Mille Lacs Band, but who lived elsewhere, opted to return "home." They came forth with documentation proving their relationship to the Mille Lacs Band of Ojibwe and were successfully added to the tribal rolls. The Band now numbers 4,300. The casinos are quite successful, and a per capita payment[8] is distributed to all Mille Lacs members.[9] As one of the most financially successful Nations in Minnesota with their gaming operations, the Band does not disclose, even to its members, how much money its casinos generate.

The first goal of the Band's 2012–2013 strategic plan, designed after extensive meetings and consultation with the whole community, is to "cherish, preserve and nurture the language, culture, traditions, teachings, and spirituality of the Band."[10] The Band members recognize that their culture is, and must continue to be, the centerpiece of their national life. Furthermore, the Band also recognizes that language is the most important of all cultural elements. Many tribal leaders and members are convinced that without language, the culture would no longer exist. Band members, Band government, and Band programs share the responsibility of assuring that every decision is based on the values they have held since the beginning of the Band's existence. Their strategies for nurturing their culture include teaching the Ojibwe language, promoting cultural education and cultural competency, preserving cultural foundations, and protecting the land.

The Ojibwe Language and Culture Program is part of the curriculum for all early education and K–12 students at the Band's two Nay Ah Shing schools. The spiritual leaders are called on frequently during various ceremonies such as powwows, funerals, births, name-giving ceremonies, and special gatherings. Elders are brought into the classrooms to offer wisdom and knowledge to preschool through high school students. The Band has two assisted living units to provide a way for elders to stay in the community and continue passing on Ojibwe culture and knowledge. Elders also serve as advisers to the Band's government, and many teach classes on traditional Ojibwe crafts such as birch-bark baskets and beadwork at the Mille Lacs Indian Museum.

The Band's Ojibwe Language and Culture Center provides a setting for Ojibwe language classes, ceremonial discussions, and other cultural activities such as wigwam construction and sugar bushing, the making of maple syrup. Many Band members continue to follow traditional hunting and fishing practices, gather wild rice, and participate in Ojibwe drum groups. Each summer, traditional drummers hold ceremonies across the reservation.

The Band invests considerably in the education of its members. Approximately $2 million is spent each year on higher education scholarships for Band members and their descendants. In the 2011–2012 academic year, about 250 students received scholarship aid.[11] The newly constructed Head Start Building opened its doors during the fall of 2012. Children learn Ojibwe and are even forbidden to speak English in some of the classrooms. The building is organized around a circle for various occasions such as ceremonies, story-telling, and dance events. Each of the three districts in Mille Lacs has indoor and outdoor facilities to hold powwows.

Between 2006 and 2012, the Band and its businesses have given more than $4 million in charitable donations to educational causes, law enforcement agencies, hospitals, food shelves, and other organizations and projects that serve local communities and the region.[12] The ability to donate to charities is one of the cultural habits that have been strengthened since the Band became more economically self-sufficient. Traditionally, Ojibwe people shared their resources with surrounding communities.[13] But the indigent living conditions they were forced into since the middle of the 1800s left little room for resource sharing.

The Mille Lacs Indian Museum offers exhibits dedicated to telling the story of the Band. It traces their journey to settle in northern Minnesota, teaches about their life before and during the treaty period (1855–1864), and follows their history up to present time. Videos, interactive computers, listening stations, and traditional objects reveal information about the Band's past and current life. The museum's spacious four-season room serves as a demonstration area for traditional cooking, birch-bark basketry, and beadwork.[14] The museum, however, is not owned by the Band; the Minnesota Historical Society (MNHS) holds the title. The MNHS and the Mille Lacs Band of Ojibwe initiated a partnership in 1996 and selected a location on tribal land, next to the tribal government center, where the old trading post was. The MNHS and the Band chose an architectural firm and agreed on the content of the exhibits. The tribe invested in the new building and contributed to the capital campaign project for the museum. The agreement is that after fifty years, in 2046, the museum shall be turned over to the tribe. The Band's and the MNHS's expectations successfully merged in a museum designed to preserve precious artifacts and incorporate the beauty of its setting to tell the Band's history.[15] A "Trading Post" is attached to it where tourists and local inhabitants alike can buy art, crafts, and souvenirs. Around 25 percent of all the articles for sale are hand-made by Native people, both Mille Lacs Band members and others as well.[16] The rest of the items for sale are either manufactured by companies that specialize in Indian art or come from businesses with famous brands such as Minnetonka and Pendleton.

White Earth Nation

With almost 20,000 members and 1,300 square miles, White Earth is the largest Ojibwe Nation in Minnesota.[17] Its members are spread throughout the state of Minnesota and across the entire United States.[18] While the Nation has ample land, their traditional Anishinaabeg language is in a state of crisis.[19]

In 2008, a study showed that there were only fifteen fluent speakers of Ojibwe in the White Earth Nation.[20] Three of those first-generation speakers have since walked on, leaving twelve in 2012, all of whom were over the age of sixty.[21] This study was one of the chief factors that led to a shift of priorities, funding, and human resources in an attempt to reinforce the Nation's history, culture, and language.

Prior to 2011, cultural revitalization was driven by families, community organizations, or individuals. There was no governmental initiative or plan in place to enhance this effort or spread the information to the rest of the Nation.[22] White Earth did have a casino generating revenue, but in the 1990s corrupt forces within the casino (including tribal leaders and outside organized criminals) negatively influenced the flow of capital resources.[23] Today casino revenue is not sufficient to fund all the services provided to the citizens of the Nation which remains reliant, like most other tribal Nations, on federal grants and funding. There are still too few funds to aid in language and cultural revitalization.

In 2010, the Tribal Council realized that coping with and fixing growing social problems such as drug abuse, domestic violence, teen suicide, and gang violence had to start with renewing the cultural, historical, and linguistic bonds, so they decided on a new course of action. As a first step, in August 2010 the Tribal Council passed a resolution that declared Ojibwe the official language of the White Earth Band of Chippewa Indians. In order to make this statement a reality, the Tribal Council knew that revitalization efforts needed structure. Their new strategic plan in 2011 contained a separate and compelling section called "Revitalize the Traditions, Language and Culture of the White Earth Nation."[24] The Traditions, Language & Culture (TLC) Committee was charged with this mission and empowered by the Tribal Council. The committee's objectives were laid out specifically in the strategic plan. They were to install language and culture into school curriculum, revise and update a book of the history and culture of the White Earth Nation, use social media and a website for language and culture enhancements, and create a video library capturing the knowledge and memories of the remaining elders. Another portion of the strategic plan encouraged the Nation to use some of the casino's profits to support these directives by showcasing White Earth Nation's traditionalists and artisans on a monthly basis, enhancing the existing casino with traditional themes and tribal elements, and hosting language classes for the community.

Total tribal expenditures in 2011 were $62 million, with culture and recreation accounting for over $1.3 million (approximately 2 percent). The Nation's General Fund expenditures, drawn from income generated through gaming revenues, grants, cigarette tax, and sales tax, were $13.1 million. Culture and recreation accounted for $1 million, or roughly 7.6 percent of those expenses.[25] The TLC Committee's direct Tribal Council funding for this first step was $20,000 in 2011, and the success of the program convinced the Tribal Council to increase its funding to $78,000 in 2012.[26] While there is no further breakdown available of how Shooting Star Casino revenues are being funneled directly into cultural and language programs, it is undeniable that, besides the TLC Committee budget above, there have been grant monies and vast human resources devoted to the culture and language revitalization in the White Earth Nation.

Fond du Lac Band of Lake Superior Chippewa

The Fond du Lac Reservation opened its first casino in 1986 and a second one in 1993.[27] The actual profit of the two casinos is confidential information that, in most cases, the Reservation Business Committee will not release.[28] However, from the anecdotal evidence available, it is a very profitable business that has provided employment to hundreds of people.[29]

The Fond du Lac Ojibwe School was founded in 1980 because of the urgent need to revive the Ojibwe language. Five of the original teachers hired at the school were Ojibwe speakers and taught the language as well as the subject matter they were selected for. Currently, Ojibwe is taught to all children who attend the school. Students who wish to expand their knowledge of both language and culture are offered after-school classes. Students are also encouraged to speak the language while sitting around the drum that is owned by the school and used for ceremonies.[30]

Additionally, the Fond du Lac Community College offers Ojibwe language courses, which are well attended. However, a concern looms that language speakers may no longer practice Ojibwe in their everyday lives after graduation, and if that is the case, the language will continue to founder. Sadly, only a few dozen Ojibwe speakers can be called fluent and hold extensive conversations in Ojibwe. In Sawyer, one of the more traditional districts on the reservation, many members speak the language, and ceremonies are still a part of life. Ojibwe is spoken at home, and some children learn it as their first language. Language tables are operated once a week in each of the communities. Generally, there is a dinner associated with the gathering, and members speak Ojibwe for the duration of the meeting.

Another way Fond du Lac Band members have proactively celebrated language is by holding immersion language camps. For the past five years, during four days in June, this camp has offered Ojibwe language revitalization and traditional Ojibwe activities on the reservation. Visitors have the opportunity to learn how to make a flute, moccasins, drumsticks, dream-catchers, and birch-bark baskets. At each station, a fluent Ojibwe speaker and a translator are present. People can also participate in canoe races on the lake or go on guided tours in the woods to learn to identify Ojibwemowin names for plants. This initiative, started in 2009 with slightly fewer than 200 people, has attracted hundreds of speakers and nonspeakers alike, amounting to 400 guests in 2010 and 500 in 2011. In 2012 and 2014, over 700 visitors attended, and in 2013 there were 1,250 attendees. This free event, open to the public, enables Ojibwe people from several states, and from Canada as well, to work with young people outside of the normal school schedule and with elders who are delighted to share their knowledge and skills. The camps have developed some quasi-fluent speakers over the years, and they answer an unmet need for people who want to practice their language but cannot find any convenient place to do so. In 2013, the budget for the camp was $32,000. Two-thirds of that amount was provided by the Reservation Business Committee of Fond du Lac.[31] This kind of contribution, which makes this exceptional four-day meeting a reality, would most likely not have been possible without casino revenue.

The Ojibwe school language program receives $85,000 per year from federal funding while the Ojibwe school immersion program receives $20,000. The language tables and ceremonies do not require funding, are voluntary, and feature potluck meals as an incentive. Most people who attend the language tables feel it would defeat the purpose of the gathering if they were paid to practice their language, which they believe should be considered an honor.

The Fond du Lac Reservation also has a cultural center and museum, which contains many traditional items. Most of the artifacts on display have been donated to the center. Unfortunately, only a very small amount of recorded history is present in the museum, and the funds to purchase additional items are not available, despite the $100,000 allocated to the museum every year, courtesy of the Nation's casino funds, which manage to cover only the cost of the basic functions of the museum; $10,000 from the same "casino/development" account finances powwows on the reservation, and a gardening club ("Gitigaan project") also receives $100,000 a year. The community centers garner $300,000 a year, and the Ojibwe speakers clinic is funded partly by the development account and Indian Health Services, with a budget of $150,000 a year.

Although the three reservations under review are different in terms of demography, location, and gaming revenues, there are similarities in the way they have each sought to revitalize tribal traditions over the last twenty-five years. The preservation of language has been carefully prioritized, the role of elders has been emphasized, and schools have been significantly enhanced to respect tribal educational and cultural standards. Even if casino revenues alone do not fund the total budget amount for all these culturally relevant programs, there is no doubt that they constitute the bulk of these much-needed funds and help communities rebuild and preserve distinctive cultural traits.

Broader Benefits to Tribal Cultures from Casino-Generated Funds

Tribal Names, Representation, and Sovereignty

In recent years, there has been much controversy, sometimes heated, about the use of tribal names or cultural images by non-Indian entities or individuals. In the past, it was uncommon to hear Natives express their frustration with the names that have been thrust upon them, the history books that have often only told the non-Indian side of events, the racist names of sports teams, and the cultural appropriation that has been threatening their identity and self-respect. Today, tribes are increasingly pointing out and resisting instances of cultural appropriation and misrepresentation. While Indian efforts to self-define are not new—neither is their awareness of the mistelling of their histories—for the longest time, conditions have not favored their resistance. Communities and individuals who are occupied with staying alive, finding sustenance, protecting their lands and building homes, accessing basic medical facilities and schools that would respect and include their cultural needs, and caring for their children and elders make difficult decisions about allocation of resources. This shouldn't be interpreted as an indication that control over one's very identity has not been of profound importance. The development of tribally owned casinos has changed conditions in a number of ways that support increasingly visible tribal control and representations of identity. Only now that their basic human needs are starting to be fulfilled can they turn to more insidious, less obvious and pervasive trends that have kept them in a perpetual psychological trauma for centuries. Tribal casinos are the object of ample media attention, much of it negative. Consequently, tribes have become skilled at managing public perceptions of their casino business and of themselves through press releases and promotional advertisements in a range of media, as well as through websites and popular social media. Casino revenues have changed two significant conditions: they provide economic breathing room so tribes can prioritize identity issues, and media attention to Indian casinos brings an otherwise ignored and marginalized community to public notice.

Alongside a growing involvement of tribes with their representation in the media, the mere—but frequent—mention of casinos in newspapers also implies that tribal Nations are under more scrutiny as well and that surrounding communities pay more attention to their demands, following closely the changes in the living conditions of tribal members thanks to casino revenue. It is not surprising, therefore, that the representation of Native Nations in the media has substantially evolved in the past quarter of a century. Significant media coverage and many more interactions with non-Indians have helped in shaping a new form of identity for Indigenous peoples. Their newfound wealth has enabled a few Native Nations to gain some leverage in the media and on political issues, which, in turn, has facilitated this raising of awareness. Here are a few examples of the changes taking place.

Native peoples have rarely been known by the names they have given themselves since time immemorial. Trying to regain this core element of their identity is a long and complex process for Native Nations. In Minnesota, the tribe popularly known as the Sioux—from the exonym "Nadouessioux" given by the Odawa and the French—call themselves the Dakota. As a matter of fact, in France people often use the word "Sioux" in a rather common expression, "ruse de Sioux," which literally means "Sioux trick," and is a laudatory and popular way of describing an ingenious plan. Similarly, the "Chippewa" of Minnesota only rarely refer to themselves by that term, preferring the use of the word "Ojibwe," although in their own language they are "Anishinaabeg."[32] During the most recent battle for treaty rights that took place in the 1990s among Ojibwe tribes, a group who defended the rights of the Indians to fish and hunt on ceded land called themselves the "Anishinaabe Liberation Front." As Jim Northrup wrote in one of his numerous columns, "it makes people aware that we are Anishinaabe. By calling ourselves that, we force the media to use the word Anishinaabe over and over."[33]

If one considers the damage that occurs on a person's subconscious when she is consistently given a name other than the one that was hers in the first place, especially by an entity that seems to have all powers over her, it is not hard to imagine what the result might be when there have been several generations of brainwashing for a whole group, whose Indian members have kept hearing that the name of their tribe was not Anishinaabeg, but Chippewa. Tribes were first subjected to an intense trauma when they lost their lands, when their population was depleted, and when their former lifestyle was threatened to the point of extinction. While Native Nations were fighting to survive physically and could barely think of a way to overcome all the obstacles linked to their history, their subconscious absorbed the reality that they were not even entitled to choose what they were going to be called and sensed that an identity theft was taking place, but lacked the tools to stop it. The reaffirmation of their ancestral names by tribes is therefore a huge step forward to regaining their identity, history, and pride.

During the last three decades, Native Nations have been better able to develop their own media, present their own interpretation of current issues, and promote their distinctive perceptions of historical events. Several recent examples demonstrate how Native perspectives have been gaining momentum. For instance, the largest mass hanging in U.S. history occurred in Minnesota in 1862, when thirty-eight Dakota were hanged, immediately following what U.S. history calls "the Sioux Uprising" but which the Dakota refer to as "the Dakota War." The Shakopee Tribe, whose Mystic Lake casino is the most successful Native business in Minnesota, has worked extensively on redefining the terms of this conflict, but also on giving another perspective on the tragic events of 1862, when the 150th anniversary of the massive hanging, which took place on December 26, 2012, gave them the opportunity to do so. Some tribes can finally seize and claim ownership of a common history that, up until now, had only been owned and told by their former enemies. Meanwhile, in northern Minnesota, the Red Lake Nation's tribal council recently voted unanimously to establish a Red Lake Nation tribal holiday, named "Old Crossing Treaty Day." This holiday will commemorate the only treaty between the United States and Red Lake Nation. Similarly, there is a current and growing movement to replace the (in)famous "Columbus Day" by "Indigenous Peoples' Day." This idea, which arose in 1977, has been gaining increasing support on a national level.

Today, thanks to casino revenue and the economic progress that has ensued, more Natives and their governments are in a better position to react publicly, politically, legally, and socially to every aspect they experience as an aggression against their culture, their image, and their identity, and they are able to fight against their cultural losses and the historical trauma they have faced. These are all critical steps toward regaining self-esteem and national pride. Tribes tend to no longer be passive when they are presented with a negative or stereotypical representation that reflects the battles their forebears had to fight to protect their descendants from a perspective that perpetuates a colonialist view of their history.

Thanks to the money casinos have generated, tribal leaders are now taken more seriously when they call financial institutions that not so long ago would have avoided their calls or brushed them aside. Tribes can also influence elections by funding the campaigns of political leaders who will be more likely to treat them as respected sovereigns. For example, Gary Goldsmith demonstrates how some Minnesota tribes have become big spenders in state elections:

> In 2006, when all state legislative and constitutional offices were on the ballot, political committees registered by Minnesota Indian Tribes with the Minnesota Campaign Finance and Public Disclosure Board spent more than \$1.2 million to influence the election of candidates for state offices. More than \$900,000 of that total was spent by the political committees of just two tribes with more than \$700,000 of that going to the several organizational units of the Minnesota Democratic Farmer Labor Party. Minnesota tribal political spending in 2002, the previous year in which all state offices were on the ballot, totaled less than half the 2006 amount, at just over \$598,000.[34]

Tribes also hire lobbyists who help get their ideas and projects heard in Washington, D.C., and help them amass some real political clout. The Congressional Native American Caucus (CNAC) in Washington gathered eighty representatives in 2013 and is one of the largest caucuses today, whereas it only used to muster a few people fifteen years ago when it was first established.[35] These political and economic advances have fostered a cultural change as well.

Charles Judd and Bernadette Park, professors in the Department of Psychology and Neuroscience at the University of Colorado Boulder, define a stereotype as "an individual's set of beliefs about the characteristics or attributes of a group."[36] Stereotypes can derive from two main sources: first, the mechanical repetition of what people have always heard their families or friends say about a particular subject; and second, several experiences that have formed a certain idea in someone's intellect, leading her or him to have a particular opinion about a group of people. Stereotypes are often born out of ignorance, misunderstanding, and misrepresentation of cultures. Thanks to casino revenue, many North American Indigenous peoples have the opportunity not only to reflect on their culture and the best ways to protect it but also to influence the very construction of the new stereotypes to which they have been subjected. How Indian tribes present their culture to the non-Indian population is critical, but more important still is how they manage to present it to their own members, building and recomposing the culture that they will choose to nurture, develop, and expose to the rest of the world.

For a long time, one of the more damning stereotypes about Indians was that they were supposed to be poor. Indeed, their citizens experienced far more poverty than the average American. According to noted author Stephen Pevar, at the beginning of the twenty-first century Natives were the most socioeconomically disadvantaged group in the United States, had the shortest life expectancy of any group, had an unemployment rate of 45 percent (ten times the national average), and had a poverty rate of almost 65 percent.[37] Along with their poverty status, a stereotype of drunkenness, a high rate of incarceration, and a frozen picture of a character "lost in translation," struggling between two worlds, two stories, and two identities, completed this typical but inaccurate portrait of Indian people.

A "new" stereotype of Indians has appeared with the advent of tribal casinos. In Minnesota, the four Dakota peoples, living closer to the Twin Cities, have completely transformed their way of living, from indigence to significant wealth. By contrast, the seven Ojibwe tribes in the northern part of the state, although much better off since they began operating their casinos, are not nearly as economically wealthy. For many Minnesotans who fail to understand the dynamics of how tribal sovereignty works, it makes no sense that a Native Nation of 20,000 members, like White Earth, cannot function the same way as another one like the Shakopee tribe, with only a couple hundred members. The general perception among many non-Natives is that today, Indians are all wealthy thanks to their casinos.

One backlash due to casinos' success is that many non-Indians who supported tribes before the gambling era did so mainly because Indians were poor and helping them meant performing a good deed. The "new Indian," however, is not nearly as poor as he or she used to be, and now not only have Native Nations lost their appeal to people who were primarily there to draw them out of extreme poverty, but they have also aroused jealousy in non-Native citizens who might not have given them a thought two decades ago. It is easier to nurture compassion and understanding for Nations that are poor and economically insignificant than for sovereigns who feel newly empowered by financial semi-independence. As Philip Deloria remarked, "Expectations underlie the objections when Native people pursue gaming enterprises."[38] Jessica Cattelino also explains that, because Indians are supposed to be poor, "poverty structures popular conceptions of indigeneity."[39] The change that takes place is unsettling to a population for whom it is reassuring to brand and frame other groups of people in specific, labeled categories. Taking it a step further, Wilkins and Stark explain that a negative stereotype currently developing is that "Indians, largely because of gaming proceeds, have become extremely wealthy and are taking advantage of federal laws to enrich themselves at the expense of the American taxpayer."[40] Once more, the lack of historical background and knowledge leads many non-Natives to misinterpret the complex and multiple changes taking place within tribal Nations.

An ongoing battle is rattling many Native Nations today as the fight against the use of words reminding them of their historical struggle against racism and disrespect is still raging, especially regarding the use of Indian names or slurs for sports teams such as the Kansas City Chiefs, the Atlanta Braves, the Cleveland Indians, and, of course, the Washington Redskins.

Suzan Shown Harjo, a forceful advocate for Native rights and the director of the Morning Star Institute, is still trying to get the message heard. The Oneida Nation—one of her most generous supporters—has funded advertisements calling on the Redskins to change their name.[41] There has also been a great effort by Indian lobbyists in Washington, D.C., to finally have the name of the team changed. The money tribal Nations are able to extend to important organizations such as Harjo's or to pay for lobbyists to do their job at the Capitol is not coming from federal programs. Casino revenue has enabled tribes to have a say on issues that used to be wholly out of their hands. It is a positive and proactive move when tribes are able to identify the immensely damaging effect that terminology can have on their own members' psyche and how words influence the perception of non-Indians around them. Stereotypes continue to adversely impact Natives, making it more challenging for them to see who they actually are or want to be. Casino money can help tribes revitalize and sustain cultural identity within their communities while educating nontribal members as well about what Indigenous cultures are and what is acceptable or not to Native Nations.

In November 2014, the Washington team came to Minneapolis to play against the Minnesota team, the Vikings. Before the game began, a rally of up to 5,000 people, Indians and non-Indian allies, gathered near the stadium to protest the name of the team. Melanie Benjamin, tribal chair of the Mille Lacs Band of Ojibwe, explained the reasons why it was important to change the racist name of the Washington National Football League (NFL) franchise:

> This word, repeated over and over, perpetuates negative stereotypes of Native Americans and contributes to a pervasive degradation of our culture and heritage. It's a reference to state-issued bounty proclamations for exterminating Indian people and providing the bloody "red skins" as proof of "Indian kill." In 1863, the

Winona Daily Republican carried the following notice: "The State reward for dead Indians has been increased to $200 for every red-skin sent to Purgatory. This sum is more than the dead bodies of all the Indians east of the Red River are worth." In the State of Minnesota, this word represents genocide, which is why so many state, university and local leaders tried to prevent it from being used at this game.[42]

These endeavors reopen the highly sensitive question of Native sovereignty. As explained earlier, tribes tend to be treated as a racial minority instead of the different *political* entity that they actually are.[43] A major risk for successful economically independent Nations is that they may face the threat of termination again, under the pretext that they no longer need the federal government's support.[44] Natives have to navigate these troubled waters with great prudence when most non-Indians have little knowledge of treaty rights and still refuse to understand that tribal peoples have a fiduciary relationship with the federal government, guaranteed through treaties—the supreme law of the land. If a change of representation can easily trigger a change in perceived stereotypes, it can also bring about a change of political agenda, which might possibly transform the current and rather progressive policy of Indian self-determination into another destructive era for tribes.

Ever since the appearance of Indian casinos and the unexpected wealth they have produced, many Americans have approached Native Nations in order to be recognized as Indians themselves, claiming one of their ancestors was Native. Of course, the goal of many of these individuals is to gain financial power, not to revel in the possibility of belonging to another culture. Tribes, by necessity, are very careful not to grant membership to anyone who cannot prove their Indian ancestry through official documents. It used to be that being Native was seen as an unfortunate fate. Unsurprisingly, more and more people are now reclaiming, or simply claiming, Indian heritage. However, tribes are not easily fooled by some people's attempts to become members, and they strive to ensure that the definition of tribal identity remains their own prerogative.

The most notable example in Minnesota is that of the Shakopee Dakota tribe, which has struggled mightily to maintain accurate membership rolls by using DNA testing. In her latest book, *Native American DNA*, Kim Tallbear explains how problematic DNA testing is as a way of identifying ancestry. According to her, "the DNA profile is increasingly used by tribes in the U.S. and by First Nations in Canada. With proof of genetic parentage, some enrollment offices allow a parent's blood-quantum documentation . . . to be invoked in order to determine an applicant's blood quantum and in turn to process that applicant's enrollment."[45] Some companies, such as DNA Diagnostic Center (DDC), even specialize in DNA testing of Natives. Even if someone is found to be part of the tribe and thus entitled to funds generated by casinos, it does not necessarily mean that they will embrace the Dakota culture. Some are likely to take the money and live their lives in another part of the world, thus destroying most of what many consider to be the fundamentals of Dakota life. Each tribe has the prerogative to define its own criteria for membership. The Ojibwe tribes of Minnesota, for example, require their enrollees to have a minimum of one-fourth of Indian blood—although the White Earth Nation is in the process of changing its tribe's specific statutes in order to be able to welcome all descendants of White Earth members as tribal enrollees. Tribes are confronted with many ethical issues concerning their enrollment and how to decide who is part of their community and who is not. Predominantly, however, they have been following the tracks—or rather, the heavily detailed instructions—left by the BIA in the 1930s, which favored a complex and mathematical calculation of the degree of Indian blood an individual possessed.

Sovereignty is intrinsically linked to the way Natives represent themselves and how they are represented by outsiders, because it influences the way they will be perceived and whether their sovereignty will be respected by others. The emergence of Indian casinos has considerably emphasized the question of tribal sovereignty. The not-so-obvious question of identity and culture defining who Indians are entails considering who actually decides "who Indians really are." It is legitimate to think that there is no clear-cut answer to such a complex interrogation when the U.S. government has over thirty different definitions of who is Indian and when tribal Nations have the inherent authority to make that decision.

Identity is a mix of innumerable perspectives and perceptions, of extremely diverse sources of comprehension and insight. The interdependence between cultures resembles the one between individuals in many respects. The members of a culture all have variable ideas regarding who they are within the greater scope of a planet like Earth, of a continent, or, in the case of tribes, of a very large united country. But the way their culture is perceived by outsiders and the very presence of different cultures around them inevitably affect the vision they have of them-selves. There is one more factor to take into account concerning Indian tribes: the successive waves of forced assimilation and acculturation that took place in their specific history. When Indigenous peoples are put into contact with a different people, they are given a choice as to whether to change and adapt their ways or to resist any evolution. If this new culture is not thrust upon them, it is more likely that their culture will evolve smoothly and without any hostile reaction to anything that does not belong to their initial civilization, probably picking here and there the aspects of the other civilization that they appreciate the most. But this was not the case of Native Americans, who have borne the brunt of a pervasive contemporary historical trauma, which originated in various aggressive and offensive federal Indian policies. Native American culture is now inextricably intertwined with the Euro-American one, and, just like blood, these two worlds can be neither separated nor quantified in a meaningful way.

It is problematic to decide what parts of contemporary Indian cultures are authentic and genuine, and what parts are some form of stereotyped folklore, fostered by popular culture or subverted by non-Indian interference. It is not even possible or relevant to tell the difference between the two when so many cultures get interwoven because of the forces of globalization. Since all cultures evolve over the years, how are Native Nations supposed to distinguish the practices that make them who they are from the ones they have to relinquish? The answer to this complex question is inevitably truncated. The prevailing solution adopted by Native Nations to define who they are—according to their perspective—is to look at their ancestors and their history, their stories and their religious values, to make sure that the essential principles of their civilization are safeguarded. However, it is impossible to say who they would be today had the Europeans refrained from colonizing their territories. If one compares the "culture" of a country like France in the fifteenth century and the way people live today in that same country, it is evident that half a millennium has considerably altered the culture of the people. Since no invader's culture was imposed on French territory, changes in culture appear to be natural and are generally accepted by the population. But Native peoples do not have the peace of mind that comes with "natural change" because change was imposed on them, although Native people did have some agency in the process and all was not forced upon them. Philip Deloria observes that "for those concerned with the integrity of Native cultural and social practices themselves, change has been almost inevitably coded as decline—as the incremental death of traditional Native culture."[46] Casinos appear for many non-Native onlookers as the epitome of such a decline of tribal culture. Nonetheless, it seems that the choice of who Indians are today and how they want to be perceived ultimately resides in their own hands and minds, although it will always be heavily influenced by the perceptions of others. This definition of identity and culture can never be a one-way street, but, on the contrary, a never-ending exchange of visions and encounters of contrasted views, which should be respected by both parties. As has been demonstrated earlier, casinos have had a major role in defining this identity, both for tribes themselves and for outsiders as well.

What Do Casinos Represent for Indians?

Indian casinos are predominantly situated on Indian reservations. This intrusion onto tribal lands of an activity whose core is based on money, when many tribal traditions are clear about the way money should be treated and looked upon—with great suspicion—creates at first an unsettling cacophony of traditional echoes amid video games' busy sounds. However, it should be noted that Ojibwe tribes and other Native societies have a long history of betting and gambling, although not associated with the capitalistic nature of casinos. After the initial doubts regarding the legitimacy of their presence on tribal soil, casinos have come to occupy a special place in Indian Country. There are several reasons why tribal members go to their casinos and enjoy spending time there.

Casinos as a Place to Gather

Many casinos include convention centers, conference rooms, concert stages, ballrooms, arcades, pools, spas, nice restaurants, and other amenities. Shows, concerts, and sporting events often take place there. It is common for winter powwows to be held inside tribal casino facilities, with enough room to receive artists who sell their traditional products before, during, or after the ceremonies or events. Tribal members also benefit from a reduced rate when they check into hotel rooms at the casino, which makes it easier to spend a weekend surrounded by family and friends to celebrate any occasion.

Given how many tribal members are related to one another, it is likely that an enrolled member will come across a relative when he or she visits the casino. The Black Bear casino on the Fond du Lac Reservation, for example, employs 50 percent or more Indian people, at every level of employment.[47] Casinos have provided jobs to reservation members, and being employed and receiving regular paychecks undoubtedly contribute to building tribal employees' self-esteem.

In some ways, casinos have become social magnets—places where people go in part because they know they will see their friends or family, and where being Indian is accepted by everyone in the facility. There is a sense of belonging that has grown at the same time as the children who have accompanied their parents and played with their friends there, then have secured their first job in a casino, and who now feel the pull of this location because it is one where non-Indians cannot make them feel out of place.

The casino belongs to the tribal Nation. It feeds the tribal citizens. It draws many members in for one reason or another. It appears to be a safe haven where being Indian in a modern society is perfectly acceptable. Casinos are also a place where it is unlikely that Indians will feel judged or demeaned by other people's stares. Non-Indians expect to encounter Indians there, and they are also on tribal land, which gives tribal members another sense of ownership and belonging. Insensitive stares and racist slurs rarely take place in casinos because the people who go there have made the conscious choice of being surrounded by Indians. In a paradoxical way, tribal casinos are the place where Indian culture and identity are at their pinnacles because their presence there is guaranteed.

The Feeling of Pride

The mechanisms at work for individual psychology also apply to larger groups of individuals. The idea that self-confidence enhances the lives of people who are incredibly lucky to have it in the first place, or those who work on themselves enough to achieve it, can be equally applied to a collective psyche. John W. Berry explains:

> Cross-cultural psychology has demonstrated important links between cultural context and individual behavioral development. Given this relationship, cross-cultural research has increasingly investigated what happens to individuals who have developed in one cultural context when they attempt to re-establish their lives in another one. The long-term psychological consequences of this process of acculturation are highly variable, depending on social and personal variables that reside in the society of origin, the society of settlement and phenomena that both exist prior to, and arise during, the course of acculturation.[48]

Most tribal members are proud of their casinos and the incredible growth they have brought to their communities. The way Native Americans perceive themselves undeniably contributes to the way others perceive them. This new self-acquired confidence in their possibilities and future has consequences on the non-Indian outlook, too.

Tribal members can ironically enjoy the satisfaction of seeing how non-Indians spend their money in the casino, knowing that their reservation will eventually be the recipient of the money gathered by slot machines and blackjack tables. Jim Northrup does not hide his optimism: "I smile when I see white people reaffirming tribal sovereignty one quarter at a time."[49] Moreover, when Indians themselves gamble, it is acceptable to lose money, since it resembles a donation to their own tribe, or a voluntary and entertaining form of taxation.

Considering that, as Philip Deloria pointed out, American history has tended to draw "from the old expectation that Indian people either assimilate or die out," it is refreshing to see how, in this instance, Indians were the ones who assimilated casinos into their own world and made them part of their redefined identity.[50]

The "Branding" of Reservations Thanks to Casinos

Increasingly, people associate reservations with Indian casinos because this business is unique in many respects. When someone says "White Earth," many people immediately think "Shooting Star Casino." Tribes never used to brand themselves in the past. When the casinos opened, Indian Nations branded these businesses, and they have been building on those brands for over a twenty-year period. Part of the tribes' marketing technique is to let the general public know who they are, that they own a business, and that they provide distinctive and remarkable entertainment one can find only on Indian land.

Raymond Brenny, chief executive officer of Red Lake Gaming, is convinced that the casinos have completely modified the representation of reservations in the American psyche:

> People do perceive the Indian reservations to be casinos. They think of casinos first, *before* they think of reservations. From my experience, in marketing and branding, we have done a very good job in branding our casinos so that people come and visit them. That brand has somewhat diminished the reservation brand. It is actually good for us, because before, there was no identity that drove the general public to focus on Red Lake or on another reservation.[51]

Economic development is imperative in order to protect and exercise self-determination. It is the first step for tribes to be able to decide who they want to be and how they desire to be perceived. According to the Harvard Project on American Indian Economic Development,

> The most commonly self-reported goals of Native Nations in the arena of economic development are *not* wealth and capitalistic riches for their own sake. Rather, Native Nations are pursuing economic development in order to have the freedom to control their own political, cultural, and social destinies and to have the ability to sustain communities where their citizens can and want to live.[52]

Therefore, the chief objective of Nations when they develop economies and businesses is far from that of becoming capitalistic Nations. Money is one of the most powerful tools for tribes to reassert their own definition of what culture means to them. According to Jessica Cattelino, "at stake in debates over tribal gaming are the value and the currency of culture."[53] Only through economic development can tribes obtain the freedom they need to control their lives and fate. But they also have to be aware of the perverse effects of such an economic activity.

As Jim Northrup remarked, "I don't think we can afford to make gambling a new Indian tradition."[54] According to Northrup, "gambling makes us think that money is everything and the only thing that is important. Respect, honor and generosity are more important in my mind."[55] Moreover, even though gaming has made a huge difference in many tribal communities—although not all—the federal government and the states are often at odds on the way Indian gaming is impacting the economy of their citizens: the U.S. government is aware that casino revenue helps develop tribes' economies and infrastructures, but states are very suspicious and often annoyed at this activity, which, in certain ways, escapes their scope, especially if there is no revenue-sharing with the state, as is the case in Minnesota.[56] For now, however, it seems to have been a constructive ally in helping rebuild tribal Nations.

Conclusion

The evidence of the effects of casino revenue on the revival of traditions, language, and customs of Indigenous communities is quite visible, despite the fact that most Native Nations zealously protect their new source of income by not publicly disclosing their revenues or the way they use them. But if one considers how quickly tribes developed cultural preservation and revitalization programs after the opening of their casinos, it cannot be ignored that the influx of money from the casinos has been the catalyst for tribes to take responsible steps toward the protection and preservation of their culture. As long as there is a sustained awareness by tribal communities and governments of the necessity to provide counseling and facilities to help people fight addictions linked to gambling, casinos can definitely be viewed as a stepping stone that will enable Native peoples to diversify their economy and become self-sufficient through various activities that will not so obviously capitalize on money and that are more in accordance with Indian cultures. For example, the Milles Lacs Band of Ojibwe purchased two hotels in St. Paul, Minnesota, in March 2013 with casino revenue, and is planning on buying many more all over the United States.

Some other benefits of gaming are not as obvious. For instance, thanks to casino revenues, tribes have been able to increase political pressure on the legislature in their respective states and in Washington, D.C., and have gained funding for culturally relevant programs or have successfully supported changes in legislation. Although they do it modestly, some casinos have gift shops that offer a wide array of Indian crafts that non-Indian customers can then be exposed to and learn about—however, more often than not, these items are made in China. Another goal of many tribes is to further develop arts and culture in their casinos by hosting ceremonies and art fairs and using the casino as a vehicle for making their history and culture known to the rest of the population.

The main question is whether the cultural revival that casinos enable is worth the cultural cost associated with possible addictions, greed, and idleness. Most tribal people welcome the possibility of enjoying their language, ceremonies, and traditions again, and it seems that regaining cultural strength through casinos is worth fighting the predictable problems that accompany gambling. However, without a built-in mechanism to counter the crippling effects of unchecked addiction, indigenous communities run the risk of perpetuating colonial oppression through gambling or chemical addiction. In order to further protect their cultures and societies, tribal nations need to direct a fair portion of gambling revenues toward traditional rehabilitation centers, to guard against the pitfalls of addiction that are endemic to a casino setting, including gambling, chemical addiction, and even food or sex addictions.

Tribally owned casinos can be powerful tools to preserve tribal culture, especially if their negative effects can be professionally managed by a combination of effective education as well as medical personnel, law enforcement, counseling programs, and self-help facilities. It is critical to the survival of tribal cultures that the people in charge of using the money generated keep in mind that the community's cultural needs are a priority and that they keep them at the forefront of their political decisions. Casinos and tribal members' lives are now inextricably intertwined. The challenging adverse consequences casinos are criticized for can hopefully be outweighed by the positive results tribes have obtained with the proactive revitalization of their community values and traditional identities. More time is needed to undo the several centuries of Euro-American brainwashing, forced assimilation, and identity suppression, and to give tribes a real chance at self-determination. People who are nostalgic about the "romanticized" Indian frozen in time seldom acknowledge the incredible cultural revival that economic development through gambling has brought to Indian communities. But the phenomenon is perceptibly taking place, and casino critics should not overlook the tremendous impact casinos are having on redefining tribal cultures according to tribes' own standards.

NOTES

1. For purpose of this chapter, traditionalists are the people who participate in ceremonies, who speak the language, and who are well-versed in their people's culture and history.
2. Jim Northrup, "Indian Gaming Exciting But May Eat Us," *Duluth News Tribune*, December 22, 1993.
3. See, for example, the arguments brought forward in Bernard P. Horn, *Is There a Cure for America's Gambling Addiction?* National Coalition Against Legalized Gambling, http://www.pbs.org/wgbh/pages/frontline/shows/gamble/procon/horn.html.
4. This classic anthropological definition of culture was provided by Julie Pelletier, a cultural anthropologist, in a personal conversation.
5. Jessica R. Cattelino, *High Stakes: Florida Seminole Gaming and Sovereignty* (Durham, NC: Duke University Press, 2008), 3.
6. These three tribes are all part of the Minnesota Chippewa Tribe and were selected because information about their cultural programs could be more easily accessed by the author.
7. Information gathered and compiled with the help of Ronald Anderson, Property Manager, Corporate Commission of the Mille Lacs Band of Ojibwe, and Curt Kalk, Secretary-Treasurer for the Mille Lacs Band of Ojibwe. The reservation boundaries were defined in the Treaty of 1855, but the county claims that a 1913 Supreme Court statement indicates that the reservation was relinquished following the 1863–1864 treaties and the

Nelson Act.

8. Per capita payments are a monthly allowance given each tribal member by the tribe. The amount of this per cap varies from $400 to $90,000 in Minnesota, according to tribes.

9. Minors' per capita payments are lower than adults', but they are undisclosed for security reasons, to protect Mille Lacs teenagers from crime, such as gang activity.

10. A copy was given to the author by the secretary-treasurer of the Band, Curt Kalk.

11. http://www.millelacsband.com/Page_FastFact_CommunityDevelopment.aspx.

12. http://www.millelacsband.com/Page_FastFact_CommunityDevelopment.aspx.

13. Jim Northrup, interview on February 16, 2014: "We were raised to believe in the old ways, we were taught how to care for each other. Being greedy was not the Indian way."

14. "Visit," Minnesota Historical Society, http://www.mnhs.org/places/sites/mlim/index.html.

15. Interview with Travis Zimmerman, Mille Lacs Trading Post and Museum Manager, September 11, 2013.

16. Interview with Shelley Foster, Mille Lacs Trading Post Sales Manager, September 11, 2013.

17. Information gathered and compiled with the help of Michael Neusser, Economic Development and Marketing Director, White Earth Nation.

18. Around 65 percent of White Earth enrollees do not live on the reservation.

19. Ojibwe people use the terms "Ojibwe," "Chippewa," and "Anishinaabeg" interchangeably, although "Ojibwe" and "Anishinaabeg" are specifically used to talk about the language.

20. ANA (Administration for Native Americans) 2008 Study.

21. When a person dies, he or she "walks on" to the next world.

22. Interview with Joan LaVoy, Director of Education, White Earth Nation, November 2012.

23. In 2010, the White Earth Band of Chippewa won an $18 million Tribal Court judgment against a Pennsylvania-based gambling company that conspired with former chairman Darrell (Chip) Wadena to steal profits from Shooting Star Casino. http://www.startribune.com/business/112191824.html.

24. Fiscal Year 2011 White Earth Nation Strategic Plan.

25. State of the White Earth Nation Program, March 2012.

26. LaVoy interview.

27. Information gathered and compiled with the help of Donald Wiesen, Human Resource Manager at the Black Bear Casino (Fond du Lac).

28. The Reservation Business Committee (RBC) is the name given by the tribe to its tribal council.

29. On October 23, 2013, 863 people were employed by the casino, 353 full-time and 510 part-time.

30. Interview with Don Wiesen, Director of Education of the Fond du Lac Reservation 1979–1989, November 2012.

31. Interview with Jim Northrup, co-organizer of the camp, May 29, 2013.

32. Ojibwe can also be spelled "Ojibway" or sometimes "Ojibwa." "Anishinabe" has many variations as well, and the same goes for "Chippewa." In Canada, many Ojibwe bands are called "Saulteaux."

33. Jim Northrup, "Mille Lacs Spearing Challenge Will Test Rights," *Duluth News Tribune*, May 26, 1993.

34. Gary Goldsmith, "Big Spenders in State Elections—Has Financial Participation by Indian Tribes Defined the Limits of Tribal Sovereign Immunity from Suit?" *Law Review* 34, no. 2 (2008): 660–61.

35. In the words of Congresswoman and current cochair of the CNAC Betty McCollum, "The Native American Caucus works to strengthen the relationships between Capitol Hill and Indian Country by providing a forum for the discussion of policy priorities important to tribal nations." "McCollum Joins Cole as Co-chair of Congressional Native American Caucus," United States Congresswoman Betty McCollum, January 30, 2013, http://mccollum.house.gov/press-release/mccollum-joins-cole-co-chair-congressional-native-american-caucus.

36. Charles M. Judd and Bernadette Park, "Definition and Assessment of Accuracy in Social Stereotypes," *Psychological Review* 100, no. 1 (January 1993): 109–28.

37. Stephen L. Pevar, *The Rights of Indians and Tribes* (Carbondale: Southern Illinois University Press, 2002), 3.

38. Philip Deloria, *Indians in Unexpected Places* (Lawrence: University Press of Kansas, 2004), 231.

39. Cattelino, *High Stakes*, 63.

40. David Wilkins and Heidi Stark, *American Indian Politics and the American Political System*, 3d ed. (Lanham, MD: Rowman & Littlefield, 2011), 214.

41. Ken Belson, "'Redskins' Name Change Remains Activist's Unfinished Business," *New York Times*, October 9, 2013.

42. Melanie Benjamin, "Change the Redskins Name," Brainerd Dispatch, November 6, 2014, http://www.brainerddispatch.com/content/change-redskins-name.

43. This was clearly addressed in the Supreme Court case *Morton v. Mancari* in 1974.

44. The Indian termination policy of the 1950s was a very controversial move by Congress to progressively terminate the United States' trust relationship with Indian tribes, starting with some of the most economically self-sufficient ones. The terminated tribes, which were not consulted, lost their status as federally recognized tribes and were to be

assimilated within the American population.

45. Kim Tallbear, *Native American DNA: Tribal Belonging and the False Promise of Genetic Science* (Minneapolis: University of Minnesota Press, 2013), 44.

46. Deloria, *Indians in Unexpected Places*, 113.

47. Wiesen interview.

48. John W. Berry, "Immigration, Acculturation, and Adaptation," *Applied Psychology* 46, no. 1 (1997): 5.

49. Jim Northrup, "New Black Bear Casino Benefits Indians, Others," *Duluth News Tribune*, June 23, 1993.

50. Deloria, *Indians in Unexpected Places*, 225.

51. Interview with Raymond Brenny, CEO of Red Lake casinos, September 20, 2012.

52. Harvard Project on American Indian Economic Development, *The State of the Native Nations: Conditions under U.S. Policies of Self-Determination* (New York: Oxford University Press, 2008), 112.

53. Cattelino, *High Stakes*, 60.

54. Northrup, "Indian Gaming Exciting."

55. Interview with Jim Northrup, March 8, 2014.

56. The state of Minnesota negotiated two types of compacts with its tribes: one for the video games of chance, between 1989 and 1991, and the other for blackjack in 1991.

"It's a Question of Fairness"

Fee-to-Trust and Opposition to Haudenosaunee Land Rights and Economic Development

Meghan Y. McCune

Stereotypes and misconceptions about Indigenous sovereignty, particularly gaming, are rampant throughout the United States and are reflected in pop culture discourses. The satirical cartoon *South Park* took up the issue of Indian gaming in 2003, dedicating an entire episode titled "Red Man's Greed" to the topic. The episode centers on an unnamed Native Nation that operates "Three Feathers Casino" outside of the fictional Colorado town of South Park. In order to grow casino profits, the Nation plans to buy and demolish South Park to build a superhighway from their casino to Denver. Upon learning of the plan, father Randy Marsh tries to comfort his son Stan and Stan's friends—"It will be ok boys. We'll just move to the next town over," he tells them. To which Stan replies, "Oh sure, until the Native Americans decide they want that land too. What if the Native Americans keep building their casinos and highways until we have nowhere else to go? We have to stand up to them now!"[1]

While the South Park situation is fictitious and the humor of the episode is rooted in the irony that it was Native Nations who lost their land to rampant U.S. economic and political expansion, in reality anti-Indian economic and sovereignty discourse deployed toward Indigenous gaming uses similar linguistic frames articulated by the fictional *South Park* characters. For example, in response to the

Cayuga Nation's request to put 125 acres into trust, local resident Gerald Masculoso told the Bureau of Indian Affairs (BIA),

> It's a question of fairness. Not to what occurred two hundred years ago, we cannot correct that. It's a question of fairness as to what will occur two hundred years hence, to the inhabitants of this particular area.[2]

Maculoso does not deny the past wrongs experienced by the Haudenosaunee (namely dispossession of land); his view places non-Native residents of the counties as modern-day victims. This sentiment is reflected in the *City of Sherrill* majority opinion;

> The wrongs of which [the Oneida Indian Nation] complains occurred during the early years of the Republic, whereas, for the past two centuries, New York and its local units have continuously governed the territory. . . .
>
> The unilateral reestablishment of present and future Indian sovereign control, even over land purchased at the market price, would have disruptive practical consequences.[3]

City of Sherrill flipped the script of Indigenous land dispossession established by *Oneida I* and *Oneida II*—the decision positioned the reestablishment of sovereign Oneida land in Madison and Oneida Counties as "disruptive," and, in essence, *unfair* to non-Native residents and non-Native governments.

In the wake of *City of Sherrill*, Haudenosaunee Nations are left with the legal hurdles of laches and disruption, which make continued litigation extremely difficult. As a result, the Cayuga and Oneida Nations have turned to the fee-to-trust process to regain or build upon land bases. Land is a crucial element for the exercise of Indigenous sovereignty, and land is also necessary for economic development. Although Native Nations can exercise sovereignty without a land base, a lack of land can put increased strain on Native governments and can stand as a barrier to economic development. For many Native communities, land, tribal businesses, bingo halls, and casinos have become practical symbols of Native sovereignty and economic self-determination.[4] As Native Nations gain economic and political power, non-Native opposition to Indigenous sovereignty manifests through anti-gaming and anti-Indian economic development discourse. Cayuga, Oneida, and Seneca economic development in western and central New York State has been met by increased opposition from grassroots organizations such as Citizens Against Gambling in Erie County, Coalition Against Gambling in New York, Citizens for a Better Buffalo, and, most notably, Upstate Citizens for Equality (UCE), a grassroots anti-Indian sovereignty organization.

This chapter contextualizes opposition to Cayuga and Oneida economic development and fee-to-trust. Specifically, I analyze gaming and land discourse directed at the Cayuga Nation and Oneida Nation through the public comments on their respective land-into-trust applications. Opposition to Cayuga and Oneida gaming is tied to opposition to land claims and recent fee-to-trust applications; additionally, both Nations operate gaming facilities in very rural regions. Even in land claim cases, contemporary anti-Indian sovereignty movements center on opposition to Indigenous economic development; a perception of "unfair business practices" is at the heart of UCE discourse and Indigenous sovereignty is framed as an affront to the economic livelihood of non-Native individuals and businesses. In essence, Haudenosaunee gaming and economic development are at the center of UCE fears regarding the exercise of Haudenosaunee sovereignty in central New York.

Fee-to-Trust and Economic Development: Gaming in Upstate New York

The 1970s U.S. Supreme Court *Oneida I* and *Oneida II* rulings opened up the federal courts to Native American land claims against states, and many Native American Nations have filed land claims throughout the Northeast to regain or build upon historic land bases. The Oneida Nation's 250,000-acre claim in Oneida and Madison Counties in New York State was the first contemporary land claim case filed in federal court.[5] In 1980, the Cayuga Nation filed a 64,015-acre land claim in Seneca and Cayuga Counties in central New York. The basis for the land claim was a series of treaties initiated by New York State beginning in the late 1700s (and consequently never ratified by Congress) that resulted in the dispossession of Cayuga land in central New York. Presently, the Cayuga Nation is the only nation within the Haudenosaunee (Iroquois) Confederacy without a land base; Cayuga Nation citizens live on Seneca and Tuscarora Nation territories, as well as in Canada and Oklahoma. Initially, in 2001, the courts awarded the Cayuga Nation over $248 million to buy land within the land claim region in order to establish a reservation.

The 2005 landmark U.S. Supreme Court case *City of Sherrill* effectively ended all indigenous land claims in the state of New York and nationwide. Here I am referring to the legal strategy employed by Native Nations on the East Coast of asserting Indigenous land rights through the 1790 and 1793 Trade and Intercourse Acts. This strategy had been successful; however, the decision rendered in *Sherrill* does not accept land claims (and corresponding assertions of sovereignty) based upon the Trade and Intercourse Acts. It is important to note that while the current legal landscape may be inhospitable to land claims, this does not mean that all avenues (legal and otherwise) of regaining land and addressing past injustices have been exhausted.

Sherrill created a new legal landscape that privileged the fee-to-trust process over land settlement—while the Supreme Court of the United States ruled against the Oneida Nation, citing concerns over checker-boarding, disruption of non-Native jurisdictions, and so forth, the majority opinion noted the option of fee-to-trust;

> Congress has provided, in 25 U.S.C. § 465 a mechanism for the acquisition of lands for tribal communities that takes account of the interests of others with stakes in the area's governance and well being. Section 465 provides the proper avenue for [the Oneida Indian Nation] to reestablish sovereign authority over territory last held by the Oneidas 200 years ago.

With little available recourse in the courts, a remaining option for regaining and expanding Cayuga and Oneida land bases is through the fee-to-trust process. Both Nations have submitted fee-to-trust applications to transfer land purchased on the open market (land held in fee simple) to reservation land (land held in trust). While this process—developed as part of the Indian Reorganization Act—is not new, the Cayuga and Oneida Nations are the only Native Nations to file fee-to-trust applications in New York State. In western New York, the Seneca Nation has used a modified process that bypasses fee-to-trust in order to expand reservation land for housing—Seneca territories in Buffalo and Niagara Falls were reacquired with Salamanca Settlement Funds.

The fee-to-trust process was developed in the 1930s under the Indian Reorganization Act. Specifically, 25 U.S.C. § 465 reads:

> The Secretary of the Interior is authorized, in his discretion, to acquire, through purchase, relinquishment, gift, exchange, or assignment, any interest in lands, water

rights, or surface rights to lands, within or without existing reservations, including trust or otherwise restricted allotments, whether the allottee be living or deceased, for the purpose of providing land for Indians.

. . . Title to any lands or rights acquired pursuant to this Act or the Act of July 28, 1955 (69 Stat. 392), as amended (25 U.S.C. 608 et seq.) shall be taken in the name of the United States in trust for the Indian tribe or individual Indian for which the land is acquired, and such lands or rights shall be exempt from State and local taxation.

As part of the process, the BIA is required to review all requests to put land into trust by federally recognized Native Nations. UCE, as well as other anti-Indian sovereignty groups, opposes the fee-to-trust process. Although the BIA addressed the legal standing of fee-to-trust in the Oneida application, some anti-sovereignty groups have challenged the constitutionality of the process in court.

A BIA review is required by the 1969 National Environmental Policy Act, which considers environmental—including human social environment—factors. The summary analysis is published in an Environmental Impact Statement (EIS); before the final EIS is completed, the public can submit comments on a draft EIS, either in writing or at a scheduled public hearing. While the main goal of the EIS is to "address the [Oneida and Cayuga] Nation's need for cultural and social preservation, political self-determination, self-sufficiency, and economic growth as [federally] recognized Indian tribe[s]," non-Native concerns are also taken into consideration. UCE has since shifted land claim opposition to fee-to-trust opposition, actively lobbying politicians, writing letters to the BIA, and organizing community members to oppose both the Oneida and Cayuga Nations' applications.

Non-Native opposition to the Cayuga and Oneida fee-to-trust applications centers around removal of land from county tax rolls and the establishment of tax-free businesses—most notably bingo halls and casinos. The Oneida Nation already operates a Class III gaming facility (Turning Stone Resort and Casino), and the Cayuga Nation has, off and on, operated two Class II bingo halls in Seneca Falls and Union Springs (LakeSide Entertainment). Gaming is a contentious issue within the Cayuga Nation. One faction of Cayuga leadership is in favor of gaming and expanding the Nation's existing gaming, while another faction strongly opposes any type of gaming enterprise. While both Nations' desire to reacquire land within their homelands is driven by more than gaming, public opposition to the process often centers on gaming. Compounding these issues is the fact that the legal foundations of gaming (and fee-to-trust) are largely misunderstood in non-Native communities.

In 1987, the U.S. Supreme Court upheld the Cabazon Band of Mission Indians' right to operate bingo games and a card club within the boundaries of their reservation (*California v. Cabazon Band of Mission Indians*, 480 U.S. 202). The ruling also served to reaffirm tribal sovereignty, as the Court decided against California's argument that its criminal jurisdiction extended to jurisdiction over gambling on reservations; this decision thereby reaffirmed tribal authority over civil matters on Indian land. In *Cabazon*, the Cabazon Band argued that Native Nations retain the reserved right to game, while California argued that gaming was a criminal matter, as it would increase organized crime and prostitution. Shortly after *Cabazon*, Congress passed the Indian Gaming Regulatory Act (IGRA) in 1988, which is essentially a "Cabazon fix," limiting Indian gaming by providing guidelines for the establishment of gaming facilities. Under IGRA, gaming is divided into three categories, with Class III gaming (slot machines, card games played against the house, and so forth) allowed only "in a State that permits such gaming."[6] Because New York State allows lottery, horse racing, and other gaming activities, federally recognized Native Nations within the state have the ability under Cabazon and IGRA to engage in gaming.

A key component of IGRA requires Native Nations seeking to conduct Class III gaming to sign a "Compact" with the state, with one stipulation—the state must negotiate in good faith with the Nation seeking to establish a casino. Under IGRA, casinos are both an exercise and limitation of tribal sovereignty[7]—Native Nations exercise economic self-determination, while still being subjected to federal and, at times, state and encroaching local regulation; encroaching state and local regulation also feeds and bolsters anti-Indian groups. IGRA aside, the *Cabazon* ruling stands as a recent affirmation of tribal sovereignty, and many Native Nations closely tie the right to operate casinos to the inherent right of tribal sovereignty and self-determination.

Several Native Nations have used IGRA and state compacting as a method to reacquire land in urban areas located in their ancestral homelands. In these areas, there are competing economic and political interests vying to control how and where Native Nations purchase land for casino development. For example, the city of Buffalo lobbied for the Seneca Nation's Buffalo Creek Casino to be built within city limits, as opposed to neighboring suburbs, but then sought to restrict Seneca hotel and restaurant development in an effort to prevent competition with non-Native businesses. While cities, towns, and municipalities debate the economic benefits of casinos, Indigenous land acquisition and economic development are often framed as "special rights" by non-Native individuals and groups critical of Indigenous sovereignty.[8] Cattelino describes this as the "double bind of American Indian need based sovereignty":

> American Indian tribal nations (like other polities) require economic resources to exercise sovereignty, and their revenues often derive from their governmental rights; however, once they exercise economic power, the legitimacy of tribal sovereignty and citizenship is challenged in law, public culture, and everyday interactions within settler society.[9]

According to this model, gaming and other forms of economic development have resulted in a "double bind" for Native governments; non-Native individuals and groups criticize both poverty and wealth in Indigenous communities and use both to advocate for termination of Indigenous sovereignty.[10] For example, in meetings in 2006 and 2007, Seneca/Cayuga UCE members consistently argued against Indigenous sovereign economic development, portraying economic development as a way to skirt taxes: "They don't need to develop. They already developed. They just want to be shielded from taxes." Or they critiqued the local economic benefits of development: "There will be no Seneca County. Ten years from now it will be like the Seneca Reservation. Desolate. There is nothing there. It's terrible."

For some Native Nations, economic development is pivotal for achieving and sustaining self-determination. However, such development necessitates increased interaction with state and local politicians and non-Native communities. In the following section, I present state, local, and Indigenous discourses surrounding Cayuga and Oneida fee-to-trust applications as well as Oneida and Seneca gaming in order to engage Cattelino's concept of the double bind as well as her 2007 call to examine the local facets of Indigenous sovereignty. Specifically, I outline examples of increased economic development by Haudenosaunee Nations that can reinforce and actively challenge aspects of the double bind. While fee-to-trust and gaming have resulted in increased non-Native opposition to Haudenosaunee sovereignty, they have also led to better understandings—and support—of sovereignty in some non-Native communities.

Illustrating the Double Bind: The Cayuga Scoping Meeting

On March 1, 2006, the BIA held a public scoping meeting to collect oral and written comments on the Cayuga Nation's fee-to-trust application for 125 acres of land in Cayuga and Seneca Counties in central New York State. A notice of the meeting was placed in local papers and communicated to county government offices in early February. Informally, UCE also advertised the meeting through its email listserve and and its monthly meeting. Approximately 500 people were present for the first scoping hearing, and over 100 submitted written and/or verbal comments to the BIA.

The hearing was held in Seneca Falls at the New York State Chiropractic College in the college's gymnasium. Large sets of bleachers divided the large gym in half, giving way to rows of folding chairs and, at the front of the gym, folding tables marked with name cards for BIA representatives. Behind the BIA representatives, a row of chairs lined the wall, designated for Cayuga representatives as well as state and local government representatives and members of the press. The rows and bleachers filled with residents of both Cayuga and Seneca Counties; save for a few Cayuga Nation members and one or two college professors, the audience was largely white and middle-age or elderly. There were a handful of teenagers and children present, sitting with their parents. Before the meeting began, UCE members greeted each other—most sitting together and some wearing UCE t-shirts. While most in attendance were prepared to speak in opposition to the application, a few people were in attendance with the goal of learning more about the issue; one Cayuga County resident told me, "I haven't heard much about fee-to-trust and I want to know how it is different from the land claim. I don't really have an opinion yet, but I would like to side one way or the other once I get some information."

The meeting began shortly after 6:30 p.m., with an opening from Kurt Chandler, the regional environmental scientist for the BIA, who introduced the other BIA representatives, including an attorney advisor from the Department of the Interior and an environmental protection specialist. Chandler briefly explained fee-to-trust:

> Taking into trust is a means that the Federal government holds the land for their fair use and enjoyment. What it does is that it makes the property tax free for the Nation, and no one can take that property away from them.

He also outlined the National Environmental Policy Act (NEPA) as well as the next steps after the initial scoping meeting;

So what we are looking for is what are the potential impacts? We will have a public comment period. And after the public comment period today, we will ask you to focus on what potential impacts we should be looking at. That's the whole purpose of the meeting, to do that. I appreciate it. Some people want to talk about, you know, a lot of different things. But please, keep your comments to what the EIS should be looking for now.

The process of drafting an EIS is uncommon and as such is new to residents of the counties. Furthermore, the process serves to position residents as victims of (unwanted) change and creates a venue for scapegoating and an opportunity for residents to echo Sherrill's notion of disruption.

The first oral comment was from Clinton (Clint) Halftown, the Cayuga Nation's federally recognized representative to the BIA.[11] Halftown addressed an audience that was overwhelmingly opposed to the Cayuga Nation's application—opposition evidenced by t-shirts (designed and printed by UCE in the late 1990s during the early stages of land claim opposition) adorned with the UCE logo, facial expressions, occasional jeering, and a few signs—most notably a mass-produced UCE sign that read "ONE NATION." When Halftown arrived in the gymnasium before the meeting began, many in the audience turned in their seats to stare as he walked to the front of the gymnasium. Two elderly women sitting in front of me remarked, "Where are his feathers?" and "He's not a real Indian."

At the outset of his prepared remarks, Halftown stated,

> I have not actively encouraged a huge outpouring of support from our Nation members, our Nation employees, or our valued customers, so that each member here could have an opportunity to speak. I am sure you are also aware that the Cayuga Nation provides jobs for residents, payments to local vendors, and value to our customers.

He continued by further acknowledging the large crowd that had gathered to oppose the application,

> In providing your comments for our application, you should base your opinion on the facts. Please do not rely on some preconceived misconceptions of what we are asking for. . . . First we are a small Nation. Very small. And the land in comparison to other Indian nations, even in comparison to other public and private land owners in Seneca and Cayuga counties [is small].

As illustrated by this statement, Halftown recognized—and sought to dissipate—fears surrounding the exercise of Cayuga sovereignty over land in Seneca and Cayuga Counties.

The vast majority of the comments of opposition were phrased with NEPA in mind; commenters mentioned topics ranging from possible impacts to the environment (land, water, air, and so forth), to potential increased demands on infrastructure and services, to an alteration of land use patterns. Most comments were directed toward concerns over the socioeconomic impact (namely, employment and income). The only topics deemed outside of the scope of the EIS were the various legal issues raised by county representatives and UCE members. The three most common themes in the discourses of opposition were economic unfairness and "special rights," concern over a "slippery slope" of establishing reservation land, and the environmental impact from economic development.[12]

The most common theme in the comments was a concern that the Cayuga Nation was exercising "special rights" over non-Natives in both counties. For example, David Dresser, member of the Seneca County Board of Supervisors (a separate entity from the city of Seneca Falls Board) and chairman of the county's Indian Land Claim Committee, questioned whether sovereign Cayuga land was necessary to preserve Cayuga culture:

> Trust status is not necessary to preserve the Cayuga culture. Instead, what we see is a tribe seeking economic advantage over non-Indians with commercial and gaming enterprises in both counties.[13]

In a similar vein, Robert Shipley (also a member of the Seneca Falls Board of Supervisors) stated,

> While we have great respect for the Native American culture, we do not believe that unfair competition with local businesses, or special rights to gambling are necessary—are necessary to preserve any culture. Furthermore, we do not believe the spirit of American equality should be circumvented to grant special privileges based on race or ethnicity.[14]

Both comments illustrate a characteristic of the double bind, the tenuous relationship between the concept of Indigenous sovereignty and that of "equality" within nation-states. Dresser argues that Cayuga culture does not need land to survive and challenges the legitimacy of Cayuga government. Shipley expresses support for Indigenous "culture," but sees economic development as separate from that culture. Whereas economic development goes unquestioned in "American culture," it is framed as a "special right" when applied to Indigenous cultures.

Citizenship is a powerful frame deployed in settler ideology. Because citizenship is contextualized within the "individual," notions of Indigenous sovereignty—a collective operating both within and yet distinct from U.S. sovereignty—challenge this conceptual structure. As Cattelino posits, "how can nation-states that commit to equality among the citizenry take account of the differential political status of indigenous peoples as citizens both of indigenous polities... and of settler states?"[15] What happens is that Cayuga rights to Indigenous citizenship are reduced to a right to practice "culture," and, as opponents argue, Cayuga culture is separated from the sovereign right to operate gaming and tax-free businesses. Furthermore, because Indigenous identity is limited to non-Native perceptions of Indigenous culture, the right to pursue economic development is placed outside of the maintenance of culture and at odds with the economic rights of non-Native individuals.

The reason why frames of "equality" and "fairness" are so powerful in discourses of opposition is because of the seemingly untenable relationship between non-Native perceptions of sovereignty and assertions of economic self-determination by Native nations. In a classic illustration of the double bind, Richard Talcott, the then chairman of UCE, argued, "The Cayuga have demonstrated their ability to open, operate, and succeed in their businesses, which meets the intentions of the IRA without trust status and negates the need for such." In his statement, Talcott frames the Cayuga not as a Nation but as a collection of individuals. As such, the Cayuga do not need sovereignty to exist, and prosper economically, as individuals; the Cayuga are so successful they do not need the perceived crutch of Indigenous sovereignty—especially when it is viewed as unsustainable for non-Native populations and harmful to local economies. Seneca Falls resident Brad Jones builds on this perspective, commenting that if the Cayuga application is approved, "this area will become a wasteland occupied by gambling parlors and social service agencies."[16] In short, Cayuga sovereignty—and perceived culture—is portrayed as not only unnecessary but also harmful to non-Native economies. To use the *City of Sherrill* frame, Indigenous sovereignty is "disruptive" to non-Native communities.

Perhaps the most common context for discussions of "fairness" is that of gaming, and as Cattelino argues, "gaming has revived need-based sovereignty."[17] As Russell Wheeler, then the vice-chairman of UCE (and now chairman), stated,

> Presently there are . . . 228 Class III gambling tribes participating in a race-based
> Congressionally sanctified—economic monopoly . . . [with] 38 states whose
> communities are imploding from escalation of the special preferential Indian
> economy created by Congress and funded by tribal contributions.[18]

In his statement, Wheeler conflates political identity with that of racial identity—
reducing the Cayuga Nation to a racial special interest group. In settler states, "racing" Native nations is a contemporary means of eroding/terminating sovereignty.[19]
Discursively, "racing" sovereign nations fits within a referentialist ideology where
the Cayuga and Oneida Nations are treated as individuals instead of as sovereign
political entities.[20] Reducing Native nations from political entities to racial groups
then makes it easier to deploy arguments of "equality" (though these arguments
are still problematic when they are race-based).

Because the double bind reduces Native nations to racial groups—by terminat-
ing political status and establishing racial/ethnic status—discourses of opposition
are often discourses of whiteness. Richard Delgado and Jean Stefanic argue that as
minority groups actively resist discrimination, dominant groups view their actions
not as steps toward equality but as an "imposition."[21] Wheeler's comments typify
two interrelated types of imposition outlined by Delgado and Stefanic: "Baselines
and Tipping Points," where reform is a "departure from a situation we have come
to regard as neutral and fair," and "The Rule and the Exception," where members
of the dominant group "view outsiders as seeking an exemption from universal
rules that all of us must obey."[22] For example, Darrell Carter, a Cayuga County
resident, argued:

> We all know that the land-in-trust issue is for the construction of casinos. No big
> surprise there. The Americans who are working or want to work at these establish-
> ments say there are no jobs in New York State that pay as well. They may have a
> point. But in my opinion, using gambling as a foundation for any state's economy
> is foolish. And if we are going down that road, it would [be] better to legalize it for
> all, and level the playing field.[23]

Whiteness changes the legal landscape as outsiders (the Cayuga) are forced to
conform to the fee-to-trust process, where their right to exercise economic sovereignty is placed at direct odds with—and weighed against the economic interests
of—non-Native populations.

As illustrated, many Cayuga County and Seneca County residents are fearful about the possible effects of the establishment of reservation status and the corresponding exercise of Cayuga sovereignty over 125 acres of land. Speakers' concerns were not limited to the current request for 125 acres of trust land (a small percentage compared to the total 64,015 acres included in the initial land claim); many residents expressed a fear that Cayuga sovereignty would spread beyond the small parcels requested in the application. As Peter Same, town supervisor of Seneca Falls, stated, "We are concerned about the Cayugas growing their reservation once land is taken into trust."[24] Same's comment again echoes the *Sherrill* frame of "disruption" and positions any Cayuga land acquisition as harmful.

As part of their model of "imposition," Delgado and Stefanic argue that the assertion of rights by minority groups creates fears in the dominant group that granting some rights will quickly snowball to more demands—a sentiment parodied in the satirical *South Park* vignette at the beginning of the chapter. This snowballing starts with the idea of imposition "through Effects and Implications," where speakers decry the assertion of rights over fears of increased demands (for example, "where will it all stop?"). Linked to this form of imposition is the argument "If You Give Them an Inch"; as Delgado and Stefanic note, "Many deployments of the imposition figure rest on a fear of the floodgates. Because the first request strikes us as extreme, the possibility of others raises real fears."[25] In his comments to the BIA, Peter Schuster, a farmer and Seneca County resident, deploys both forms of imposition;

> The 125 acres doesn't sound like very much—out of 55,000. But it's like the camel getting his head in the tent. They are not going to stop. A few years ago, they propositioned me for my farm. It's 300—about 300 acres for a casino. Now I can't think of anything worse to be facing the environment than replacing my strawberry patches with a casino.[26]

Even though the Cayuga Nation did not outline any plans for a Class III gaming facility, speakers at the scoping meeting viewed the initial request as so extreme that it validated their fears that even more extreme changes would ensue from a Cayuga land base.

While there are many factors that influence fear and opposition toward Cayuga sovereignty, some opposition is rooted in a disconnect between stereotypes of Indigenous Peoples and a perceived reality. For example, John Saeli, a resident of the town of Varick, said,

This fee to trust thing, you think about the Indians, you see it on TV, clear water, fresh water. It isn't about water. It isn't about clean land. It's about money. Gambling. For crying out loud. Gambling casino. People go in, this LakeSide Entertainment, you talked about, it isn't entertainment. It's dirty. It's filth.[27]

In this case, the Cayuga Nation does not fit Saeli's idealized image of the "noble redman" stereotype, best typified by Iron Eyes Cody (a non-Native actor who made a career playing Native Americans in film), of Indigenous Peoples living off the land with minimal environmental impact.[28] This sentiment exists within UCE, where a clear distinction is made between "traditional Cayuga" and those Cayuga who want to pursue gaming—while both are regarded as an "imposition," expanded Cayuga economic development is regarded as the greatest imposition. The stereotypes of the "gaming Indian" and the "traditional Indian" are played off each other in opposition discourse, and both stereotypes of Indigenous Peoples are at the heart of Cattelino's double bind.

Contemporary Indigenous/settler relations in the United States are complicated by new forms of economic development and postcolonial assertions of sovereignty. Kevin Bruyneel argues that the disconnect between Indigenous economic development and non-Native conceptions of Indigenous Peoples influences public opposition: "By succeeding economically the tribes temporally outpaced their claim to sovereignty, while still being seen as somewhat alien to American political life."[29] Because Cayuga sovereignty is viewed as an "alien" concept and because non-Native residents occupy a marginal position in the neoliberal state, thus experiencing economic insecurity, Indigenous assertions of sovereignty are viewed as a "Fear of Loss of Control:" "All of us derive part of our self-definition from the wider society. Thus on some level we understand that radical changes in our surroundings could change us as persons."[30]

After all of the county politicians and leadership of UCE had a turn to speak, Rich Ricci, a former Seneca County chairman of the land claim committee and UCE member, approached the microphone to address a panel of BIA representatives.

You expect us to roll over and [accept] the settlement. We will not. We won in the courts. You expect us to welcome the sovereign Nation that does not play by the same rules. You expect the hard-working taxpayers to pay more. You expect our businesses to compete when they cannot. You expect one group to obey the laws of this great nation, and another not. We will not stand for the balkanization of this land. . . . One final thing, while I have eight seconds. I hope it wasn't against the law. You come into this auditorium. What comes out of this hearing will affect generation after generation, and you do not have the courtesy to salute the flag. So I ask all of you to stand up now and salute it. I would like to say the Pledge of Allegiance.[31]

At this point, all but a handful of the auditorium's 500-plus attendees rose from their seats, faced the large U.S. flag hanging from the east side of the gymnasium, and recited the Pledge of Allegiance, shouting the words "one nation" with particular emphasis. Ideas of citizenship and American identity are central to UCE's discursive frames and illustrative of the identity its members perceive as under threat. The pledge, recited at UCE meetings and public events, is a consistent assertion and defense of this identity. The pledge, coupled with Ricci's statement, embodies all of the discourses of imposition; the Cayuga are framed as an economic threat (as well as a threat to individual identity within the settler nation-state)—an entity that does not play by the rules and places an undue burden on the non-Native residents of the counties. In other words, the Cayuga are too powerful economically and thus should not be able to exercise sovereignty over land in Cayuga and Seneca Counties.

Although an overwhelming majority of speakers channeled their preexisting economic concerns into opposition of Cayuga sovereignty, a small handful of speakers, including two employees of Cayuga Nation Enterprises and an anthropology professor from Wells College, articulated the potential economic benefit of Cayuga sovereignty. Richard Kidder, a Seneca Falls resident, spoke of the declining tax base and loss of manufacturing:

Creating new industries and business in Seneca County hasn't happened in over 40 years. The last was I.T.T., Goulds Pumps is on its way out. And like it or not, a casino is going to be built here. It should be built here. It would provide hundreds of construction jobs." He continued, "As far as it being a casino and gambling: Look around. Every convenience store in town has a Lotto machine. You go into a restaurant and a bar, they have Quickdraw. There is an [Off Track Betting] up the street. They just put slots in a racetrack up in Farmington. So gambling is here. And like I said, it's about—all I ever wanted to say other than we should at least look at the casino being built there instead of another area where they would get the jobs and benefits.[32]

Kidder's comments do not fit neatly into the double bind; in the context of the EIS, he positions Cayuga sovereignty as having a potentially positive socioeconomic effect on the counties—one of the few entities willing to invest in the region. Additionally, Kidder reframes the argument of "equality," noting that the state currently operates gaming; this statement positions the Cayuga Nation as a sovereignty entity—like states, not individuals. Statements like this begin to complicate the double bind; Kidder frames gaming activities not as "special rights" but as rights already exercised by other governments (in this case, New York State).

The Cayuga Nation does not presently operate a Class III gaming facility and its economic enterprises are small. As a result, the Nation's economic visibility is limited and subject to speculation and fear. Under these conditions, the opposition to Cayuga land into trust fits well within Cattelino's double bind. However, a different framework was deployed by non-Native residents to the east in Oneida and Madison Counties. While the Cayuga discourse centered on individualism, "special rights," and a clear double bind, the Oneida public discourses deployed the frame of Haudenosaunee sovereignty and positive economic development.

Rethinking the Double Bind

The Oneida Nation submitted its application to the BIA to put 17,370 acres of land into trust in April 2005. A draft EIS was made available to the public for comment and two hearings were held, on December 14, 2006, and February 6, 2007, to collect oral and written comments. The final EIS addressed common concerns ranging from loss of property taxes to whether the Oneida Nation could legally use the fee-to-trust process. Unlike the Cayuga hearing, the majority of public comments were in favor of the Oneida's request to place land into trust. The Oneida case provides an example that challenges the dominant double bind and construction of Indian-ness that pervades dominant non-Native thought.[33] Although UCE is active in Oneida and Madison Counties, the majority of county residents work either directly or indirectly for Oneida Nation Enterprises. Driving through Oneida and Madison Counties at the height of land claim and sovereignty opposition was visually different from Cayuga and Seneca Counties—visible signs of land claim opposition were rare in the towns and villages that surrounded Oneida Nation businesses.

When I attended the December 14, 2006, Oneida fee-to-trust draft EIS public hearing at the Stanley Theater in Utica, UCE members were clustered in a small group near the front of the theater, and the audience was a sea of red T-shirts, distributed by the Oneida Nation, which read "My Job, My Vote." One after another, non-Native residents and employees (often one and the same) addressed the BIA in support of the Oneida Nation's application to take over 17,000 acres into trust. One of the most common concerns was the potential loss of employment if the application was not approved. The EIS addressed this concern and noted that if Turning Stone Resort and Casino was closed, along with other Nation businesses, "there would be a significant loss of 5,265 jobs affecting the 86 percent of workers (or 4,556 residents) of Madison or Oneida Counties who are directly employed or indirectly supported by the Nation's economic activity."[34] This concern was reflected in many of the public comments; speakers addressed the declining manufacturing base in central New York, and some even chronicled their history of employment at companies that have since closed or moved out of the area.

A number of the speakers in support of the application were small business owners—suppliers to the Nation's businesses who emphasized the economic impact of a sovereign Oneida Nation for off-reservation, non-Native businesses. Pat Castello, president of the Mohawk Valley Building Trade Council, stated:

> The expansion and development of the Turning Stone Resort and other Oneida holdings has been one of the few bright spots for the construction industry over the past 10 years. There was a time when the only construction cranes—I mean not tearing things down, but building things—from Buffalo to Albany were located at the Turning Stone Resort.... There was times when there were over 400 construction workers on-site working, sometimes perhaps close to 500. That's 500 families that are getting health care, pensions benefits and paychecks. Employees or construction workers are a benefit to our region, they spend their paychecks locally. They buy automobiles, they take their families to dinner and they buy clothing and support local charities. They are a driving force in the economic well-being of Central New York.[35]

Some speakers expressed distain for UCE and fear about a potential loss of Oneida employment. Robert Wielt, a Casino Services Department employee, proudly told the BIA, "I don't have a job anymore, Mr. Chairman, I have a career. This is an amazing opportunity and responsibility I'm truly proud of. And I owe it all to the Oneida Nation." Wielt addressed the handful of statements against the proposal from UCE members,

Mr. Chairman, there is a group of very outspoken people who call themselves Upstate Citizens for Equality, who want to crush the Oneida Indian Nation, close down their businesses and put 5,000 people out of work. That is their stated objective. Mr. Chairman, the UCE does not represent my interests nor those of my family. I implore the BIA to do the right thing here. If the UCE gets their way it would be a monumental disaster, a horrific nightmare, a catastrophe of truly epic proportions. There will be only one Turning Stone ever, please don't let them kill it.[36]

Where Cayuga and Seneca County residents were fearful of the economic impact of a sovereign nation, Madison and Oneida residents expressed anxiety over the repercussions of a loss of tribal sovereignty. In fact, in Wielt's statement, the Sherrill/UCE frame is reversed, and it is UCE—not the Oneida Nation—that is "disruptive."

In fact, Oneida Nation employees pointed to UCE as the cause of many of the tensions. Dale Romleski, a Turning Stone employee, addressed the comments of UCE Oneida Madison chapter president directly:

Mr. Vickers stood up here and said that there is no racism involved. You're right, it goes way beyond racism. I am not Oneida Indian but yet every day for the 10 years I have worked for Oneida Nation I face harassment, criticism, threats, picketing. And it's all because of where I work, not because of the color of my skin, but because I work for the Oneida Indian Nation. . . . As you sit here and listen to the comments of those stating that land trust could only make it impossible for local and state governments to function, I simply remind you of the benefits that Turning Stone has brought to your community. If bettering your communities makes it impossible for you to function, then it is only because you refuse to adjust to change.[37]

Another Turning Stone employee, Vincent Lercara, directed his comments to UCE and accused UCE and county officials of wasting time and money on court cases;

Can you recall a time in recent years that our elected officials have saved 5,000 plus jobs? The Empire Zone is a program that offers free money to companies that are interested in building, functioning and/or relocate to this area for a predetermined period of time. However, once that time has expired and the company is to start payment in addition to taxes, ironically these companies desert our area. Thus causing massive unemployment and financial hardships and a feeling of discouragement among citizens.[38]

After going over the allotted three minutes, Lercara's time was cut off; at the very end of the evening he was allowed to return to the microphone, and he said to Vickers, "You claim to be the President for Upstate Citizens for Equality. What equality are you fighting for exactly?"[39] Both Romleski and Lercara reverse UCE frames of economic victimization and equality, identifying the Oneida Nation and non-Native residents as victims of anti-Indian sentiment. This victimization is tied to a larger economic threat where UCE is now identified as the disrupter, potentially eliminating thousands of jobs through its attacks on Oneida sovereignty.

Comments like Lercara's acknowledge the double standard applied to Native businesses; New York State implemented "Empire Zones" beginning in 1999, which offer a temporary tax-free status to businesses that relocate to struggling regions. Groups like UCE that include tax equality in their platforms do not address non-Native businesses that receive tax-free status. Helen George, an Oneida Bingo Hall employee, pointed out the disjoint in UCE tax rhetoric, "Why do you suppose that everyone isn't screaming and running around about the tax breaks they're offering to these other businesses? How come it isn't a disastrous problem then that's going to put us all in the poor house?" She continued,

> If you close our casino down you're going to have 5,000 people on unemployment, collecting food stamps, on Medicaid, depressed and hopeless. We will be stuck in a hateful situation. No jobs, we can't afford to move out of the state to work because nobody is going to want our homes. Who wants to live in an area where there is no work and no future? We are in an extremely vulnerable position. If you don't place the Oneida Nation land into trust you will be destroying our lives and our futures.[40]

George's statement is another example of a reversal of UCE frames; instead of scapegoating the Oneida Nation for the region's economic insecurity, she posits that a potential lack of jobs and declining real estate value would be linked not to the exercise but to the elimination of Oneida sovereignty. Again, UCE is positioned as "disruptive" in this reversal.

The Cayuga case illustrates that economic insecurity can result in scapegoating and subsequent attacks on Indigenous sovereignty—even when that sovereignty comes with proposed economic development. However, Oneida and Madison Counties have experienced positive economic growth and employment from years of Oneida economic development. As a result of a positive economic shift directly influenced by the Oneida Nation, many residents such as Cesar Valdez Jr., security director at Turning Stone Casino, confront the double bind head on:

> As great as this country is we are not perfect. There are some folks that refuse to accept the prosperity of the Oneida Nation, they would like to see them back on the reservation in a state of poverty, in a state of despair. Please be honest, racism is alive and well. Not in everyone, but in a good percentage of folks that resent that it is not they who have prospered.[41]

Valdez acknowledges the economic growth of the Oneida Nation and the Nation's relative power as compared to other entities in the region. However, he does not frame this economic power as a result of "special rights" or a "threat" to non-Native business. Rather, he accuses critics of the Oneida Nation of racism. For Valdez, economic success is not a reason to erode Indigenous sovereignty.

It was not just Oneida Nation employees who directly challenged the double bind while speaking in support of the application; Bob Larson, who identified himself as a "taxpayer, landowner, and veteran"—a typical frame used by members of UCE—argued,

> Some have said that we would not have to close down all of the businesses, only the casino. This is a brilliant idea. I can see the tourists flocking to the hotels located in the middle of the corn field. I can also see the PGA proudly announcing to America the kick off of their fall tour located at "that place down the road from the big cow. . . . Beyond taxes it is obvious to me and to many others that there are those among us whose sole purpose it so discredit the Nation. They do not want to see Indian people get ahead of them in any way. This is pitiful. The only thing I can think is worse is when the rest of us listen to them and allow them to take the lead.[42]

Like speakers before him, Larson flips the typical UCE frame of "victimization" and argues the economic threat to the region is not the Oneida Nation, but rather those who seek to challenge and eliminate Oneida sovereignty. In a similar vein, Peter Day, president of Day Wholesale, Inc., spoke about the benefits to suppliers:

> My point is that the Nation has positive far reaching economic benefit for off-reservation business located in New York State. . . . An old saying in the tourism business is that "A rising tide floats all boats." With the Oneida Indian Nation what is good

for the Oneidas is good for all of New York State. In summation, the Oneida Indian Nation is not looking for a handout from the federal government or New York State. They just want to be left alone and unhindered while they pursue their quest for economic development for their Nation and their people.[43]

The above quotes demonstrate how non-Native residents and employees discursively complicate the double bind; the above speakers do not "race" the Oneida Nation (even while accusing UCE of racism), and Indigenous sovereignty is not framed as a "special right" doled out by the federal government and "unfair" to non-Native businesses and individuals, but rather something that makes the Oneida Nation autonomous from state and federal governments. In other words, the Nation is portrayed in an idealized capitalist frame—operating with wealth trickling down to local non-Native populations.

Conclusion

As a result of UCE goal displacement after the dismissal of both the Cayuga an Oneida land claims, opposition to Haudenosaunee economic development is now front and center in UCE's fight against Indigenous sovereignty. While Cattelino's double bind provides a helpful framework for analyzing many non-Native responses to Indigenous economic development, the Oneida case in particular provides examples of how to successfully challenge the double bind without compromising Indigenous sovereignty. The Oneida fee-to-trust case study illustrates that mutual economic interests, a vision of a shared future, and Native and non-Native connections to land and place complicate the traditional double bind.

Instead of merely complicating the double bind, some non-Native residents see more of a shared future with the Oneida Nation than New York State. As a result, the traditional double bind is dismantled, and instead of calling for Oneida termination, some residents go so far as to call for New York State termination. Brenda Sears, Utica resident and vendor for Turning Stone and other local businesses, stated, "And I really think—you could give all of New York to the Oneida Indian Nation and they would do a beautiful job with it."[44] With that said, the Oneida model may not apply to Native nations across the United States; such challenges to the double bind might only be applicable to economically struggling regions where a Native Nation's development results in increased non-Native employment; but those characteristics apply to central and western New York, where many Haudenosaunee Nations have faced challenges to their sovereignty.

Successful reframing of "sovereignty" and a reversal of UCE frames in Oneida territory most likely would have similar success in Cayuga territory, which is also a rural area with a need for increased employment and economic development. The process of reframing is important for Haudenosaunee Nations, and for those who support Indigenous rights and self-determination; countering UCE discourse and contemporary judicial termination of Indigenous sovereignty depends on rethinking the traditional double bind that pervades non-Native interpretations of Indigenous peoples. Although the double bind greatly influences how non-Natives conceptualize sovereignty (legally and locally), the Oneida example provides insight into the potential of reframing sovereignty. Such reframing does not just benefit Native Nations but can also reduce local conflict and expensive litigation, and help Native and non-Native communities work together.

NOTES

1. *South Park*, "Red Man's Greed." Comedy Central Broadcast, April 28, 2003.

2. U.S. Department of the Interior, *Cayuga Indian Nation of New York Environmental Impact Statement Scoping Report Conveyance of Lands into Trust Cayuga and Seneca Counties* (New York: U.S. Department of the Interior, 2006), 39.

3. City of Sherrill v. Oneida Indian Nation of N. Y., 544 U. S. 197 (2005).

4. Jessica R. Cattelino, *High Stakes: Florida Seminole Gaming and Sovereignty* (Durham, NC: Duke University Press, 2008); Steven Andrew Light and Kathryn R. L. Rand, *Indian Gaming and Tribal Sovereignty: The Casino Compromise* (Lawrence: University Press of Kansas, 2005).

5. Arlinda Locklear, "The Oneida Land Claims: A Legal Overview," in *Iroquois Land Claims*, ed. Christopher Cecsey and William A. Starna (Syracuse, NY: Syracuse University Press, 1988).

6. David H. Getches, Charles F. Wilkinson, and Robert A. Williams Jr., *Cases and Materials on Federal Indian Law*, 5th ed. (St. Paul, MN: Thompson West, 2005); Light and Rand, *Indian Gaming and Tribal Sovereignty*.

7. Light and Rand, *Indian Gaming and Tribal Sovereignty*.

8. Jessica Cattelino, "The Double Bind of American Indian Need-Based Sovereignty." *Cultural Anthropology* 25, no. 2 (2010): 235–62.

9. Ibid., 235–36.

10. Ibid.

11. At the time of writing this chapter, a faction of the Cayuga Nation is challenging Halftown's status as a federally recognized representative. The BIA has not weighed in on the leadership dispute, choosing not to recognize any leader until the dispute is solved internally within the Nation. At the time of this scoping meeting, Halftown's leadership had already been challenged within the Nation.

12. U.S. Department of the Interior, *Cayuga Indian Nation of New York Environmental Impact Statement*.

13. Ibid., 43.

14. Ibid., 26.

15. Cattelino, "Double Bind," 241.

16. U.S. Department of the Interior, *Cayuga Indian Nation of New York Environmental Impact Statement*, 37, 46.

17. Cattelino, "Double Bind," 248.

18. U.S. Department of the Interior, *Cayuga Indian Nation of New York Environmental Impact Statement*, 48.

19. Joanne Barker, "For Whom Sovereignty Matters," in *Sovereignty Matters: Locations of Contestation and Possibility in Indigenous Struggles for Self-Determination*, ed. Joanne Barker (Lincoln: University of Nebraska Press, 2005).

20. Jane H. Hill, *The Everyday Language of White Racism* (West Sussex, UK: Wiley-Blackwell, 2008).

21. Richard Delgado and Jean Stefancic, *Critical White Studies: Looking Behind the Mirror* (Philadelphia: Temple University Press, 1997).

22. Ibid., 101.

23. U.S. Department of the Interior, *Cayuga Indian Nation of New York Environmental Impact Statement*, 64.

24. Ibid., 36.

25. Delgado and Stefancic, *Critical White Studies*, 101.

26. U.S. Department of the Interior, *Cayuga Indian Nation of New York Environmental Impact Statement*.

27. Ibid., 90.

28. Raymond William Stedman, *Shadows of the Indian: Stereotypes in American Culture* (Norman: University of Oklahoma Press, 1982).

29. Kevin Bruyneel as quoted in Cattelino, "Double Bind," 247.

30. Delgado and Stefanic, *Critical White Studies*, 102.

31. U.S. Department of the Interior, *Cayuga Indian Nation of New York Environmental Impact*

Statement.

32. Ibid., 99.

33. Cattelino, "Double Bind"; Philip J. Deloria, *Playing Indian* (New Haven, CT: Yale University Press, 1998).

34. U.S. Department of the Interior, *Final Environmental Impact Statement Oneida Nation of New York, Conveyance of Lands into Trust* (New York: U.S. Department of the Interior, 2006), 15.

35. Ibid., 106.

36. Ibid., 139–41.

37. Ibid., 186–88.

38. Ibid., 193.

39. Ibid., 216.

40. Ibid., 99–101.

41. Ibid., 90.

42. Ibid., 94.

43. Ibid., 157–59.

44. Ibid., 177.

Masking Anishinaabe *Bimaadiziwin*

Uncovering Cultural Representation at Casino Rama

Darrel Manitowabi

Arrive at the casino [Rama]. It looks amazing, like an Aztec temple rising out of the darkness. I am amazed. So are the other people in the shuttlebus. One white woman to my right marvels aloud at the aboriginal paintings decoratively placed on the side of the building, "Pretty native, eh?" How quintessentially Canadian.

—Drew Hayden Taylor, *Further Adventures of a Blue-Eyed Ojibway: Funny, You Don't Look Like One Two*

Located in the Chippewas of Rama First Nation in south-central Ontario, Casino Rama was the only Aboriginal commercial casino in the province until 2011.[1] Officially opened in 1996, the casino is rich in Chippewa/Anishinaabe cultural representations in order to stress the Indigenous context of the casino. As the quotation above by Canadian Anishinaabe humorist Drew Hayden Taylor indicates, for the visitor of the casino, these representations explicitly mark the casino as being rooted in Indigenous Anishinaabe cultural representations. To the critical scholar, it would appear as a commoditized indigeneity of what Robert Berkhofer Jr. referred to as the "Whiteman's Indian," in reference to stereotypical Indigenous imagery.[2]

On the other hand, there exists a competing articulation of indigeneity within the community. In 2002, the community established the Culture and Research Department to promote culture and identity in the community. The departmental expression of culture is a nonmaterial, interconnected social experience best described by the Anishinaabe term "*bimaadiziwin*." The following is a comparative examination of commercial casino representations with community expressions of culture via *bimaadiziwin*. This chapter is based on twenty-four months of anthropological fieldwork conducted at the Chippewas of Rama First Nation from 2002 to 2004 and six months of additional part-time research on Casino Rama in 2011. This methodology involved semistructured interviews, participant observation, and detailed observation of Anishinaabe self-representations at Casino Rama. In the following, I suggest *bimaadiziwin* is an accurate expression of Anishinaabe culture while the casino images serve marketing interests that conform to non-Indigenous expectations of indigeneity. To accomplish this, I provide a background of Casino Rama, review the literature on Indigenous casino cultural representations, and provide a background of the Chippewas of Rama Culture Department.

Background

Though the Indigenous peoples of North America have a long history of gambling that dates to pre-Columbian times, commercial Indigenous casinos in North America are a relatively recent phenomenon.[3] Their contemporary emergence dates back to U.S. tribal bingo operations in the 1970s leading to the passage of the Indian Gaming and Regulatory Act (IGRA) in 1988 and the subsequent proliferation of tribal casinos.[4] In Canada, the development was similar: bingo operations in the 1980s led to casinos in the 1990s.[5] In Ontario, casinos were conceived as economic engines to address socioeconomic disparities, and the U.S. experience served as a model. The Chiefs of Ontario, a provincial body representing all 133 First Nations in Ontario, initiated discussions regarding the establishment of one casino in the province to benefit all First Nations in Ontario via revenue distribution and casino employment opportunities. At the time, the then New Democratic provincial government was also exploring provincial casinos to address a recession. Upon learning of the Chiefs of Ontario's intentions, the province entered discussions with the group. The New Democratic government strongly supported Indigenous self-determination and, in turn, agreed to support a one-casino concept. This support was strategic in order to ensure that provincial casinos and the First Nations casino would not compete with one another. In 1993, the province and Chiefs of Ontario reached an agreement that one First Nations casino would be established in the province and all First Nations would share its revenue. Thereafter the Chiefs of Ontario invited all First Nations to submit their proposals to host the casino. Of the fourteen submitted, the Chippewas of Rama were selected as the host community because of location, their experience with tourism, and community support. Casino Rama opened on July 31, 1996.[6]

The literature on casinos tends to focus almost exclusively on the topics of Indigenous-state relations, sovereignty, social and economic impacts, gambling problems, and Indigenous empowerment.[7] There is a limited literature on the issue of self-representation of Indigenous culture at casinos, and this is primarily limited to a handful of studies based in the United States; there are no Canadian-based studies. In the following I summarize this literature and indicate how my study contributes to the literature on Indigenous casino representations.[8]

The literary scholar Mary Lawlor, who examined tribal self-representations in museums, powwows, and casinos, undertook the first study on this issue. Specific to her casino studies, Lawlor compared self-representations at casinos and museums belonging to the Mashantucket Pequot and Acoma Pueblo.[9] At Mashantucket, the Pequot only recently regained tribal status in 1983 and opened a casino in 1992.[10] Lawlor found a similar narrative of self-representation at the Foxwoods Resort Casino and Pequot Museum and Research Center. The museum's focus is on a Pequot historical past illustrated by a diorama of a sixteenth-century Pequot village and ending with contemporary displays of its people. The casino is dominated by essentialist representations such as these: waitresses dressed as "Indian maidens"; imitation trees and rivers; a majestic statue of a warrior named "Rainmaker" who is on one knee, looking skyward with a bow and arrow drawn and pointed to the air; sounds of drums and eagles; and generic pan-Indian motifs. Though most of the representations are essentialized, there are some limited contemporary representations such as a photograph of an elder adorning one of the casino's entrances, and a space that displays some materials from the museum, profiling artifacts and contemporary community photographs. Lawlor characterizes the museum as "serious" while the casino is "playful." For Lawlor, the two feed each other; the casino is an economic engine that fuels the "nation building" taking place at the museum wherein tribal members are investing in revitalizing their culture and identity.[11]

At the Acoma Pueblo in New Mexico, Lawlor compared the museum and village tour with their Sky City Casino. The museum is filled with historical and cultural artifacts, with pottery dominating. The village bus tour is a narration of the Acoma settlement history from the thirteenth century to the present. Like the Pequot casino, the Acoma Pueblo casino is filled with U.S. popular Indigenous cultural representations of the Southwest, such as geometric designs on carpeting; pueblo-style architecture; animal, arrow, and thunderbird petroglyphs on tiles; and imitation rock and waterfalls. For Lawlor, both sets of representations are striking, and she spoke with a tribal leader who acknowledged the Acoma have lived in two worlds for several centuries. Within this framework of understanding, the casino is strictly economic, and many Acoma do not patronize it, but rather see it as a business that benefits the community.[12] On the other hand, according to her tribal leader informant, the Acoma envisage sovereignty as a framework for tribal representation.[13] Ultimately for Lawlor, the public displays function as a "displayed withholding," meaning they function as a public skin or face for non-Indian audiences. Thus popular cultural motifs at casinos conceal private tribal issues such as cultural revitalization at Mashantucket or tribal sovereignty at Acoma Pueblo.[14]

The Mashantucket Pequot Museum and Foxwoods Resort Casino are also the focus in a case study by anthropologist John Bodinger de Uriarte.[15] With its abundance of photographs and diagrams, his analysis brings to life the earlier descriptions by Lawlor. Rather than repeat these descriptions, I focus on the author's contribution. Bodinger de Uriarte characterizes the casino as economic capital and the museum as symbolic capital contributing to the nation-building of the Mashantucket Pequot. Most of his focus is on the museum, which he sees as a counterhegemonic narrative of the Pequot disappearance, thus affirming the continuity of a Pequot presence in Connecticut.[16] He suggests that Foxwoods, like other Indigenous casinos, uses mainstream and essentialized representations along with modern self-representation as a way to engage in its own "performative identity politics," thus destabilizing the image of the Indian. In this model, the Pequot subscribe to essentialized imagery to satisfy expectations of indigeneity, though they manipulate this by integrating contemporary self-representations that do not subscribe to expectations of pan-Indian imagery. Essentially, the Pequot are Indigenous actors manipulating the logic of capitalism for tribal gain.[17]

My third and final review, by Cuillier and Dente Ross, analyzed 224 U.S. tribal websites and critiqued self-representation as a mechanism for promoting tourism.

Eighty-six of the tribes examined have casinos; thus the authors were able to determine if casinos had any impact on the type of representation employed.[18] The researchers coded self-representation into three categories: historic relic (for example, the Whiteman's Indian stereotypical images); voiced participant (for example, modern life portrayal and some references to a mythical past); and informational (for example, primarily neutral text). In their analysis the authors found that tribes with casinos tended to rely on historic relic and informational material. In contrast, those without casinos tended to focus on informational material with minimal reliance on historic relics.[19] The authors conclude that casino tribes are more likely to represent themselves as historic relics rather than voiced participants. To quote one example from a tribal Oregon casino website, it "deliver[s] the message of non-Indians escaping from the dominant culture to the pastoral, carefree, natural world of the noble savage."[20] The authors suggest that the main motivation of the tribes is to appropriate the Whiteman's Indian image as a strategy to attract visitors and increase economic power, although in the process, stereotypes are perpetuated.[21]

This literature represents the limited studies examining Indigenous cultural self-representation at casinos. There are other related studies that I will briefly mention. In a literature review of selected Indigenous tribes with casinos, Comaroff and Comaroff focus on a critical approach to some tribes that regained tribal status once IGRA was passed. For the Comaroffs, these tribes are "commodifying descent" and employ Indigenous descent as a form of "ethno-capital" to capitalize on casinos in neoliberal times.[22] In another study examining television depictions of "casino Indians" on four U.S. television programs, Lacroix found that they are portrayed as both the ignoble savage of the past and a continued threat to mainstream Americans because of their increased economic and political power.[23]

My study continues the examination of Indigenous cultural representations at casinos with community self-representations and has elements in common with both Lawlor's and Bodinger de Uriarte's studies. However, this study is unique since it focuses on Anishinaabe self-representations, both externally and internally, and is based on lengthy anthropological fieldwork. In both the aforementioned studies, museums are intended for both public and private (tribal) audiences. In my study, I compare the external cultural representation of the Anishinaabe with an internal self-representation of Anishinaabe culture intended for a private Indigenous audience.

Anishinaabe Self-Representations at Casino Rama

For the visitor to Casino Rama, the depictions of Anishinaabe art, symbols, motifs, language, and architecture are readily apparent. These cultural representations are the product of the Mnjikaning Art Studio, a consortium of Chippewas of Rama members who came together in response to a call in 1995 for artistic work to be featured inside and outside the casino.[24] The exterior of the casino is covered with large-scale murals inspired by local history and by Anishinaabe scholar and spiritual leader Eddie Benton-Banai.[25] The art wall at the casino was designed through community consultation, resulting in the decision to feature the seven clans of the Anishinaabe as the major theme of the casino. The Chippewas of Rama artists followed a clan model, each sharing equally in the designs and execution of the art.

The dominant clan of the casino and community is the deer clan, which represents community caregivers and artists.[26] Deer images appear throughout the casino and are prominently featured on the casino sign with the "o" in the word "casino" in the shape of a sun with a deer in the middle.

The second clan at the casino is the bird clan, and represents the community spiritual leaders. More specifically:

> They are considered educators, gathering the seeds of knowledge so they may be spread over all the Earth. Of all our birds, the Eagle flies the highest and thus volunteered to be the link between the Anishinabe people and the Creator. Mishoomis Mgizi (Grandfather Eagle) presides over the birds and is the spiritual head of the family. His wings extend in a protecting embrace of the sky above the world of human beings and his eyes see all.[27]

In the mural of the bird clan, Grandfather Eagle wears a breastplate signifying the protection of the sky, while the eagles, ducks, and blue jays act as guardians. Grandfather Eagle's wings carry night into day.

The third clan on the casino wall is the marten clan, representing the warriors and protectors. This clan symbolizes love for the community and is the first to offer help, even defending against attack if necessary. The mural of the marten clan on the wall has hands, symbolizing help and care. Two martens are shown, one representing the warrior and the other representing generosity.

The fourth clan represented is the crane clan, responsible for such roles as leadership, external affairs, and intergovernmental relations. In the mural of the crane clan, a portrait of a community member who played a vital role in traveling to casinos and researching their impact is celebrated in the center. As well, Chief Yellowhead, a famed leader of the past, is portrayed.[28]

Honored in the fifth mural is the loon clan, symbolizing chiefs and internal affairs. Known for their oratorical ability and communication skills within all clans, the role of the loon is to have knowledge of the local environment and internal dynamics of the community. In this particular mural, another past chief of the community, Chief Big Wind, is represented.

The sixth clan is the fish clan, referring to the philosophers. This clan is connected to leadership; its members have roles as mediators, stargazers, and visionaries. The mural depicts a cross section of Lake Couchiching and its fish and fish weirs.

The seventh and final clan shown is the bear clan. The bear symbolizes the medicine gatherers and protectors; it has an understanding of land and nature and thus has the ability to harvest herbal medicines for healing. In modern times, the bear clan is responsible for policing the community, and in the mural, a portrait of the founders of the Rama police department is at the center.

In order to attract and retain more gamblers, on September 18, 2002, a 289-room luxury hotel opened. A highlight of the hotel is its 17,000-square-foot multimedia rotunda, located in part of a walkway connecting the casino and hotel.[29] The rotunda features four colors: yellow, red, black, and white. These colors symbolize the four colors of humanity: Asians (yellow), First Nations (red), Africans (black), and Europeans (white). At the center of the rotunda, a timber structure forms a circular fish fence, symbolic of the Mnjikaning fish weirs. Above the center, on the ceiling above it, there is a giant video screen bordered with a sweetgrass medicine wheel. Surrounding the giant center ceiling video screen are seven vertical video screens. On the floor surrounding the rotunda are eight tree columns representing the Anishinaabe clans: deer, bear, crane, loon, bird, martin, and fish, as well as a final column representing Mother Earth. The video screens display a multimedia presentation of Rama's cultural history with state-of-the-art lighting and surround sound. A digital image is displayed on each tree column, making each appear to be alive and speaking. Without the digital image, each replica tree is a rough carving. Footprints from each clan are illuminated in the floor at staged intervals.

Within the presentation, viewers are informed that the fish weirs predate the Egyptian pyramids and that the Chippewas of Rama have maintained their weirs for the last few hundred years. It is revealed that the Creator called the fish to hold a council at the narrows between Lakes Simcoe and Couchiching, informing the people how to build the fish fence weirs. The images of the weirs serve as reminders to give thanks to the fish that sacrificed themselves for food. The rotunda symbolizes the planet Earth, the ceiling represents the sky, and the ground represents earth and water. The presentation also includes a recitation of the creation story of the Anishinaabe, revealing that the earth was once covered by water and that the Creator called upon the turtle to form land. The muskrat successfully brought earth from the bottom of the water to form the earth on the turtle's back. Animals in the rotunda are shown diving, searching for earth that eventually formed on the back of the turtle.

Aside from the creation legend, prophecy abounds in the rotunda story. One prophecy relates two opportunities for the Rama Anishinaabeg to tell their story. In the first instance, the Anishinaabeg would tell their story, but would not be understood. In the second, another opportunity would arise, and the four colors of humanity would be drawn to the community, ready to listen. It is then recited that elders state the time is now. Further, the clans are introduced, along with their respective functions. The final symbol, Mother Earth, reveals the importance of women, especially ensuring that community issues be addressed and that the appropriate leaders be chosen.

At the base of the hotel is the Weirs Restaurant. From the exterior, the restaurant appears as if it is encapsulated in a giant weir. Painted on the ceiling are fish, while on the interior walls appear the fish inhabiting Lake Couchiching. As well, abstract artistic renditions of fish adorn the walls. Within the restaurant are images reflecting the natural surroundings of Rama. For instance, Rama is on the cusp of the Canadian Shield; thus, rock images are displayed within the restaurant and at other parts of the casino. Across from the Weirs Restaurant is the Firestarter Lounge. At its center is a huge fireplace with three sides, representing the Three Fires Confederacy of Ojibwa, Odawa, and Potawatomi Anishinaabeg. Along the walls are beaded images representing the community's artistic heritage. Behind the lounge bar are black-and-white photographs of community members.

The hotel is built in the shape of an elongated historic Anishinaabe lodge, and throughout, paintings, murals, and symbolic images abound. Most of these symbolic images are made of wood, rock, and water, replicating nature. The entrance to the casino has a replica limestone bedrock formation with a waterfall. The entrance is framed by a squared timber structure; ceiling windows allow natural light to shine in. The floor is made of replica stone with animal and "Indian" motifs ingrained.

In the lobby, stone seats and replica stone formations are in the shape of a turtle, yet again evoking cultural symbolism. The carpeting in the hallway connecting the casino and hotel contains the Seven Teachings of the Anishinaabe. Near the hotel elevator there is a large mural depicting drumming, featuring

> The story of the drum. Two drummers in the centre sing to call the clans together. And on the outskirts, the clan animals are seen to be moving toward the centre as they are moved by the rhythm of the Heart Beat of Mother Earth.
>
> Chippewa tradition says if we can find this rhythm we will find ways to work together. In the building of Casino Rama, for example[,] the people of Mnjikaning have shown they are responding to the call of the drum and are beginning to reclaim their destiny.[30]

Inside the gaming space there is an abundance of motifs woven into the carpeting. A huge dreamcatcher hangs from the ceiling in the center. Alongside portions of the inside walls of the casino, replica animals are perched at the top, and the sports bar has hand-drawn pictograph stick-figure motifs engaged in various activities such as lacrosse, skiing, and hunting.

Chippewas of Rama Culture Department

When I first arrived at the Chippewas of Rama First Nation, I was asked to assist in the development of the Culture and Research Department. I thus observed the community express culture. It was expected that this department would ultimately play a role in the development of a cultural center or museum. As a pathway to this goal, research began to document the culture and history of the community.[31] Beyond this, it was expected that the department would work with all aspects of the community, especially the education sector and youth.

I actively embraced this role with a community member who had initiated the process prior to my arrival. I arrived in June 2002, and by October 2002 we had officially secured a space at the community center, the Mnjikaning Arena Sports Ki (MASK), a building attached to the elementary school, housing an ice rink, fitness gym, and community hall for the newly created Culture Department. In September 2002, a secretary was hired; by January 2003 a new manager was hired; and by April 2003 a cultural coordinator was hired. As a researcher, I maintained my connection with this department and knew intimately the mechanics of its involvement in the community. My role was limited to helping and, when necessary, facilitating the functions of the department. Its activities were driven by suggestions by community members and an advisory committee. I followed a grounded theory approach in my research and did not arrive with the explicit goal of documenting what the Culture and Research Department did, but merely documented the organic processes that took place in the community.

The Culture and Research Department works with all aspects of the community, including its political leadership, internal administrative units (social services, education, health, elders, recreation), and external relations with regional First Nations and organizations. When the department formed, it was decided language revitalization would be a priority. It was further decided that an elder advisory committee be formed to advise and monitor language activities. During its first two years of operations, the department undertook the following initiatives: cultural teachings in the school (for example, significance of the powwow, maple sugar, hand-drumming); an after-school drum program; community powwow coordination; cultural liaison and awareness for the surrounding region; opening ceremonies for public gatherings; craft nights; language classes; developing language learning material; coordinating trips to cultural events (powwows, ceremonies) and a community history project.[32]

The department also served an important social function. Many community members, both on and off reserve, dropped by the department to visit. When I left in 2004, these activities were expected to continue and diversify, based on the changing needs of the community.

The department worked with all aspects of the community and adapted to the existing First Nations' political and organizational structures. For example, the local school is federally funded and uses the curriculum established by the province of Ontario. Only limited language instruction is integrated into the curriculum. A formal Indigenous-based curriculum does not exist, nor a budget to accommodate extended instruction in culture and identity. The Culture and Research Department offered to provide the school with free instruction and free materials, and requested only an accommodation. The principal was more than happy to cooperate, and the department thereafter provided biweekly cultural teachings for students from kindergarten to grade eight. The teachers were extremely grateful and observed that students looked forward to these classes; even "problem" children seemed to behave themselves.

It would appear that some activities of the Culture and Research Department mimic the essentialized and esoteric Whiteman's Indian, such as "drumming" and "powwow singing." My observation, however, is that these activities mask an important social and cultural expression of indigeneity. These activities are first and foremost social events that function as an opportunity for community members to gather, visit, and tell stories. Drumming, singing, and making crafts are conduits to the socialization and sharing of cultural expression. During most evening events, children played around and both men and women exchanged gossip and stories. This took place while men practiced powwow singing and women engaged in craft-making. In this sense, singing and drumming were superficial activities while stories of the past and present played a central role.

Despite the apparent success and value of the department, not all members of the political leadership were always supportive. Some were influenced by Christianity and were skeptical of a "tradition" that they interpreted as a competing religion.[33] Others considered "hunting and fishing" to be real culture, not activities such as "drumming" and "dancing." Others were supportive, while some remained neutral. The department was formed despite obstacles, and when I was in the community, there were still political leaders who remained indifferent. After the department was established there was some debate whether the support was genuine; at times, there were rumours that the political leadership would terminate it.

Despite the fact that the political leadership did not fully support the department, the opposite was true of the community. Elders were happy to share stories and help with language revitalization. Youth enjoyed learning about their culture and identity. Teachers at the school enjoyed the opportunity to enhance the learning experience of the students. Thus members of the Culture and Research Department were active with all age groups within the community and even to some extent outside of the community. The department was active in all social events and allowed the community to provide a foundational basis for direction and action. It was a conduit for community action. This appears to be how the community expresses culture: take advice from the elders (representatives of the past), advise and help all members of the community (the present), and invest in educating the youth (the future). The department is the only structure created in the community without any input or restrictions imposed by the province or federal government. The only exception is that its operations rely on income generated by the casino.

When I left the Culture and Research Department in June 2004, a community member was hired to undertake the research role I was responsible for. From then until the present, I have kept in touch with members of the department. At present it maintains some of its original activities but is now only staffed by a coordinator and a researcher.

As part of my research at Rama I was interested in uncovering the Indigenous cultural logic that informed the creation of the Culture and Research Department. While I was collecting community narratives comparing the past and present of the Chippewas of Rama, three elders provided insight into this logic. While reminiscing on the past and comparing it to the present in an interview, one elder stated:

> We've come a long way with so many changes and it's sad to know that these fun events no longer exist the way they used to [yearly fish fry, New Year's feast]. The people loved fishing and trapping because it was one of many ways to help feed each other. There was always the sense of togetherness while growing up in this community. When I went to school we were never allowed to speak our Native tongue at all. If we let our Native tongue run wild, we would get in trouble by the teachers. This community and its people never had a whole lot back then, but we did have each other and we survived the rough times together. Everyone in the community seemed happy to be involved with one another especially when we got together on special occasions. Yet many things have changed [for example,] who we are over the years. We are no longer as close to one another as we used to be. It would be wonderful to see history repeat itself and bring back that closeness for the sake of sharing with our future generations.[34]

In a separate interview conducted with two elders, both reminisced about past times while conversing in Anishinaabemowin.[35] A portion of their dialogue follows:

> *Gii feast wiiyan every New Year's Eve* (We used to feast every New Year's Eve), *kina gaa biidot miijim* (all brought food), *kina go yaawat binoojiiyak* (all the children were there).
>
> *Miikwenman niisa'iing halling pine go mnozmawe* (I remember down in the [community] hall, they always cooked).

The second responded, "*Aapja go gii bamaadziyaa* (We all lived a very good life)."[36] What is striking in this dialogue is the statement, "*Aapja go gii bamaadziyaa,*" meaning "We all lived a very good life," to describe to social centeredness of the community. The first elder is concerned with the decreased sociability of the community with the introduction of the casino. The second group of elders mentions group meals and community visiting as elements of the "good life." This suggests that such social activities contributed to a positive sense of community well-being. Central to this statement is the term *"bimaadziyaa,"* meaning "living life," or, expressed as a noun, this term is *"bimaadiziwin,"* meaning "way of life." Before I discuss this further, I first briefly review some of the substantive literature on Anishinaabe *bimaadiziwin.*

Anishinaabe *Bimaadiziwin*

Various scholars have examined *bimaadiziwin* as the key to Anishinaabe ontology and epistemology. There is comparative research on the culturally related Cree equivalent, but since my focus is on the Anishinaabe, I concentrate on this literature.[37] In the last decade I have observed a significant rise in the literature on Anishinaabe *bimaadiziwin.* In the following I review what I consider to be the most substantive examinations on this term.[38]

The first academic to document *bimaadiziwin* was the anthropologist A. Irving Hallowell, based on his fieldwork on the Lac du Flambeau Anishinaabe of Wisconsin and the Berens River Anishinaabe of Manitoba. Influenced by the "Culture and Personality School" in anthropology, Hallowell was concerned with issues of acculturation and cultural experience and explored the modal personality structure of the Anishinaabe. Based on his assessment, Hallowell concluded,

> The central value of aboriginal Ojibwa culture was expressed by the term *pimādazwiwin*, life in the fullest sense, life in the sense of health, longevity, and well-being, not only for oneself but for one's family.[39] The goal of living was a good life and the Good Life involved *pimādazwiwin."*[40] A key element in acquiring *pimādazwiwin* was the help of a spiritual helper and depended on socially appropriate behavior.[41]

The Anishinaabe scholar and spiritual leader James Dumont has also explained the meaning of *bimaadiziwin* from an Indigenous perspective. For him, an individual is walking a predetermined path in life, a path defined prior to birth by the grandfathers (or spiritual beings). The Midewiwin Lodge reflects the path of life and is constructed in an east–west direction in seven sections.[42] Each section represents the seven stages of life: good, fast, wandering, truth, planning, doing, and elder. The good life is associated with purity and birth. The fast life represents adolescence, a time of fasting and changing and seeking direction, while the wandering period represents a period when youth are in search of maturity. The truth involves the period when a young adult finds meaning, and the planning stage occurs when the individual has a family of his or her own, repeating the cycle of life. The doing period occurs when individuals act on the fasting vision and fulfill their purpose in life. The elder is at the zenith of existence in this world and is a source of guidance and knowledge.[43]

Reflecting upon his fieldwork experience in the Algonquin Anishinaabe community of Pikogan in Quebec, the sociolinguist Roger Spielmann concluded that a respect for nature, the Creator, and other people is central to *bimaadiziwin*. According to him, "*Bimaadiziwin* is virtually impossible to translate accurately in English. Each time I asked bilingual Anishinaabe people for a translation, they seemed to agonize over the problem, and every translation was a bit different."[44] Common translations include: "a worthwhile life," "a long, fulfilling life," "our walk in life," or "walking the straight path in this life." Spielmann interprets these to mean that central to *bimaadiziwin* is living a balanced life with respect to family, community, other-than-humans, the environment, the Creator, and the spirit world.[45]

A recent explanation of *bimaadiziwin* by Anishinaabe scholars Leanne Simpson and Edna Manitowabi concludes that it is an Indigenous theoretical framework for decolonization rooted in tradition and stories.[46] For these authors, the Indigenous essence of being exists as a personal connection to stories and the performance of ceremonies. It is possible to link teachings in the creation story and life cycle to one's own life as a guide to living a good and balanced life.[47]

In sum, this selective review of literature on *bimaadiziwin* reveals its link to the past of the Anishinaabe as an ontological framework of social relations among humans and nonhuman animal beings and spiritual beings. Key to this framework is an understanding of balance and respectful behavior in the context of these complex social relations. Spielmann best sums up the key elements: a respect for family, community, the environment, and spiritual beings.[48]

Discussion and Conclusion

I begin my discussion with an experience in the field. In the summer of 2002, soon after arriving at Rama, I attended a public community meeting. There I was introduced to a noted artist, powwow dancer, and follower of Anishinaabe teachings and traditions. We spoke a bit about powwows and art, something I know enough about to sustain a conversation, and when the community meeting started, I decided to sit next to him to continue our conversation. At one point in the meeting, the economic development manager at the time provided an update of economic activities to date. This individual was a non-Aboriginal person who spoke of job creation, the casino's success, and opportunities for further economic growth. Throughout his presentation, the artist heckled the manager, yelling, "Bullshit," and to his remarks about job creation he yelled, "Yeah only if you have blond hair and blue eyes!"[49] Though I felt a bit uncomfortable, I noticed fellow community members did not interfere. I left this meeting thinking that there was a tension in a casino driven by change and some of the community.[50]

The broader context of this tension came to light when I spoke with two other community artists who were involved in creating some of the artwork in the casino. One remarked to me that he was contracted to create artistic symbols and was not fully made aware of how they would be used. The Seven Teachings taken from Edward Benton-Banai served as inspiration for these symbols. The contracted artwork was then extended to carpets without the artist's knowledge. He did not know his work was going to be used in this way and felt he should have been consulted, especially since countless gamblers walk on his creation every day.[51]

After spending some time in the community I realized a collective tension existed between the original artists involved in creating the cultural representations at the casino and those involved in building the casino. As I have indicated, the Mnjikaning Arts Studio was formed in response to a call to decorate the casino. I further learned that the studio was given physical space to work from, and all supplies were provided. The studio's viewpoint was taken into consideration when the casino was being built, and my sense is the artists felt they were active participants in its development. Once the casino was built, this relationship ended and a new tenuous relationship emerged between economic developers and the artists.

With the casino construction under way, in 1995 community members were commissioned to "decorate and beautify the gambling facility inside and externally [and] artists were interviewed and screened."[52] It is thus clear that actors involved in building the casino explicitly intended to create a casino having a particular "Indigenous appearance." Interviewing the artists ensured those favoring these objectives were recruited. Furthermore, once the work began, the major influence were themes from Benton-Banai's book on Anishinaabe culture and traditions, and the inclusion of local history (for example, the fish weirs and historic chiefs and leaders), the place (Canadian Shield rocks, animals, and species of fish), and the language. In a community publication produced by the political leadership of the community and Casino Rama, the section on the background of the casino states, "Casino Rama is a magnificent structure which takes pride in portraying the proud culture and traditions of Ontario's First Nations people."[53] My research reveals a complexity behind this statement, and it is here that I begin to compare the Anishinaabe representation at the casino and at the Culture and Research Department.

The casino solicited artists of Rama to submit their suggested symbolic representations of the Anishinaabe. These commissioned symbols serve as the basis of what visitors see as "indigeneity." This is necessary since the casino was originally marketed as an "Aboriginal casino"; hence visitors expect to see aboriginality. Ultimately the casino markets symbols that are of the "traditional and cultural" type. With the exception of the photographic collection in the Firestarter Lounge, the symbolism is comprised of feathers, words, motifs, replica waterfalls, wood, dreamcatchers, talking trees, clans, turtle shells, and many other symbols representative of an essentialized timeless Anishinaabe culture associated with nature.

On the other hand, *bimaadiziwin* is, in many ways, the opposite. Most members of the Chippewas of Rama do not identify with the culture presented at the casino. For instance, very few actively identify with their ancestral clans. Though there are efforts at language revitalization, at present the language is only spoken by a few over the age of fifty. As well, though some members participate in ceremonies, they represent only a minority. Most do not see a connection or understand the constructed Anishinaabe self-representation at the casino.

However, although many do not explicitly mention their clan, all community members have a strong association with family. Families remain important, and gatherings are held within them. Aunts and uncles are secondary mothers and fathers, and cousins are secondary siblings. Thus, most behave as though they are part of a clan. With this point in mind, I found that members of certain families shared similar traits. Some families were more culturally conservative, or "traditional," in the sense that they actively sustain their ceremonies and married within the Anishinaabeg. Some families had histories of leadership, while others were generally well respected, and others were determined and aggressive. Thus, in this sense there is an informal role and responsibility for families, similar to that of the clan system, though roles are not defined in the same way that they are in the casino mural.

In contrast to the casino, the Culture and Research Department is drawn from the inner experiences of those who created it. The Chippewas of Rama Anishinaabeg did not copy an existing culture department; they merely created an image of what they perceived culture to be. I compare this to Merleau-Ponty's analogy of the painter who works in "full innocence," seeking a "science" in art, and this is "fundamental . . . perhaps of all culture." Merleau-Ponty uses "birth" to identity this process, and in his analogy, "The painter's vision is a continued birth."[54] Like Merleau-Ponty's painter, the Culture and Research Department does not practice a lettered culture or a culture learned at college or university. Members of the department are simply practicing a continued birth of *bimaadiziwin*. This cultural practice and experience meet the needs of the community and act as a medium for community being and becoming.

The anthropologist Tim Ingold has drawn inspiration from the work of Merleau-Ponty, the work of A. Irving Hallowell, and Colin Scott's work on the Cree equivalent to *bimaadizwin*.[55] He borrows Scott's term "continuous birth" as best describing Anishinaabe relational epistemology as symbolic of a person's movement along life's path, all the while drawing on an internalized understanding of the world that is projected outward and experienced as a part of relationships where the collective behavior is structured on a collective cultural model.[56]

As I have demonstrated, Anishinaabe *bimaadiziwin* does not exist in a vacuum. About 1 kilometer down the road is a casino that depicts culture in ways that are best described as the Whiteman's Indian evoking a timeless connection to nature. Even the process reveals a non-Indigenous model. I found strong tensions between the artists and allies of the artists in the community, and community members involved in the casino development at the business end. Casino developers built a relationship with Anishinaabe artists with the explicit intention of extracting Indigenous ideas and concepts for economic purposes to market an "Indigenous" casino.

To shed some additional light on this, I provide an example from my fieldwork experience. On September 18, 2002, the hotel and rotunda officially opened, and as a part of this opening, the Chippewas of Rama community members were taken on a tour of the new hotel and presented with the rotunda show. I attended this event and observed that many were impressed with the Anishinaabe-inspired architecture and Anishinaabe-inspired artwork. The rotunda show both captivated the community and was, at times, humorous, a process that I call a mesmerizing "digital storytelling," like an extravagant powwow fancy dancer, the rotunda light show, and talking clans described earlier. The humor came about when community members who acted out the clan roles were profiled as "talking trees," with their digital facial images projected on a tree, providing clan teachings. It was humorous because members were "acting" or "playing" "real Indians." These individuals are average community members and do not espouse a projected aura of overt Indigenism, thus all knew this show was not "real," but merely a "show" designed for non-Aboriginal visitors. One community member, a bit embarrassed at seeing himself, laughed with everyone else and left the event saying it was "just for fun." My observation is the community members understand that the images and the rotunda show at the casino are for casino visitors and the casino is an economic engine, thus they do not take it seriously.

So what is one to make of all of this? My answer to this is influenced by Mary Lawlor's work, cited earlier, especially her engagement with the terms "displayed withholding" and "public skin" as a reference to the essentialized Indigenous representations at the casinos she visited. I am also here influenced by Berkhofer's concept of the "Whiteman's Indian" and Frantz Fanon's concept of a "Black skin, white masks."[57] To make this connection, I briefly summarize their ideas.

Lawlor examined dual self-representations of U.S. tribal groups, comparing casinos and museums. She found that casinos incorporated essentialized cultural representations of Indigenous peoples, though at tribal museums, Indigenous peoples actually experience and project localized expressions of indigeneity. In this model, the casino is the "public skin" concealing an internalized expression. She engages with Berkhoher's Whiteman's Indian to describe the constructed image of Indigenous peoples portrayed as threatening and violent, or noble and one with nature. Ultimately, these projections are a by-product of the colonial relationship, wherein Indigenous peoples must be imagined and experienced as "other" or "inferior" to justify subjugation. The work of Frantz Fanon on the psychopathology of black people living in white societies has relevance to Lawlor's "public skin." Fanon examined the colonial domination of blacks by whites and the psychology of racism. From the perspective of blacks, in such an environment, an inferiority complex emerges, based on white society's inscribed cultural representation of blacks as being violent. Fanon uses the image of a mask to allude to this duality.

Situating this existing literature within my study, it is clear how Casino Rama is the "public face" or "mask" of Anishinaabe cultural representation, while the

Culture and Research Department is its "private face" for non-casino eyes since activities are only open to community members. Casino actors and artists willingly and actively created a projected image of the Anishinaabe. Building on Fanon's work, there appears to be a collective psychology at work here. Both casino actors and Anishinaabe artists *knew* the representations needed at the casino since the casino imagery is based on the dominant society's conception of Indigenous cultural representation. This explains why the artists created the kind of work they did and were complicit in the process.

On the other hand, when the Culture and Research Department came into existence, the community members of the Chippewas of Rama *knew* the *actual* cultural reality as experienced by the *non-casino* Anishinaabe. This reality is best expressed by the indigenous concept of *bimaadiziwin*, a shared worldview and experience that puts the individual, family, environment, and spiritual beings at its core and is understood by all members of the community, regardless of the level of their knowledge of clans, language, and ceremonies. In essence, the casino Anishinaabe representations "mask" Anishinaabe *bimaadiziwin*. In the process, indigeneity is misrepresented to serve an economic purpose. The Rama Anishinaabeg negotiate this misrecognition and transform the resulting economic gain to revitalize their culture and identity based on an Indigenous way of knowing and being: *bimaadiziwin*. Hence, like Drew Hayden Taylor's quoted non-Aboriginal visitor to Casino Rama, the artistic images serve non-Indigenous expectations of indigeneity, and, in the process, they conceal an Indigenous expression of indigeneity that is invisible yet persists as a continuous virtual birth shared in stories and Anishinaabe social centeredness that has existed from time immemorial.

NOTES

1. The terms "Chippewa" and "Ojibwa" are variant pronunciations of the term "*ocipwe*," meaning "puckered up," referring to a style of moccasins. "Chippewa" is the term of preference in the United States and southern Ontario, and "Ojibwa" is used in the rest of Ontario and Manitoba. See Edward S. Rogers, "Southeastern Ojibwa," in *Handbook of North American Indians*, vol. 15, *Northeast*, ed. Bruce Trigger (Washington, DC: Smithsonian Institution, 1978), 763. In their language, the Chippewa refer to themselves as the Anishinaabeg (plural) or Anishinaabe (singular). This term has various spellings and translations, the most common translation being "human beings." Depending on the dialect, "g/k" are interchangeable, the "g" representing the southern Ontario dialect. See,

for example, *The Chippewas of Mnjikaning First Nation: A Proud Progressive Community* (Rama, ON: Mnjikaning First Nation, n.d.). In Canada, the Constitution Act (1982) recognizes "Aboriginal" as referring to "Indians, Inuit and Metis." This term is commonly used in government and academic circles. Increasingly the term "Indigenous" is replacing the term "Native" to reflect the global experience and articulation of the colonization of original peoples worldwide. In Canada, the "Indian Reserve" is now generally replaced by the term "First Nation" in response to decolonizing efforts at recognizing Indigenous peoples as the original or first nation of Canada. In the United States, the terminology generally used is "Native American," and the word "tribe" is the term applied to the group. I will use the common terminology used in Canada and the United States, though when comparing both groups I capitalize "Indigenous" to recognize these peoples as being legitimate and equal to groups such as "Europeans." Prior to the casino, the First Nation in question was referred to as the "Chippewas of Rama," and in 1993 the name was changed to the "Mnjikaning First Nation" since *"mnjikaning"* means "place of the fence" and refers to archaeologically-significant fish weirs at the narrows between Lakes Simcoe and Couchiching, bodies of water adjacent to the First Nation. See *Chippewas of Mnjikaning First Nation*, 4–5. This name change divided the community and eventually the First Nation informally modified its name to "Rama-Mnjikaning" (a term in use when my PhD was completed in 2007). In 2008 the community held a referendum and voted to revert to the "Chippewas of Rama." See "It Is the Chippewas of Rama," Chippewas of Rama Community Forum, April 7, 2011, http://chippewasoframacommunityforum. blogspot.ca/2011/04/it-is-chippewas-of-rama.html.

2. Robert Berkhofer Jr., *The Whiteman's Indian: Images of the American Indian from Columbus to the Present* (New York: Vintage Books, 1979). For a comparative Canadian critique, see Daniel Francis, *The Imaginary Indian: The Image of the Indian In Canadian Culture* (Vancouver: Arsenal Pulp Press, 1993). Berkhofer and Francis posit that the image of the Indian is created by mainstream Americans and Canadians and serves an ideology grounded on the subjugation of Indigenous peoples. The Indians are presented as either noble savages or bloodthirsty, but always inferior.

3. See Kathryn Gabriel, *Gambler Way: Indian Gaming in Mythology, History and Archaeology in North America* (Boulder, CO: Johnson Books, 1996). For a comprehensive North American overview that includes the Anishinaabe, see Stewart Culin, *Games of the North American Indians*, vol. 1, *Games of Chance* (Lincoln: University of Nebraska Press, 1992). For a brief Canadian overview, see Diamond Jenness, *The Indians of Canada* (Toronto: University of Toronto Press, 1977), 158–60.

4. My intention here is to focus on casino cultural representation, and thus I will not

provide an overview of the history of U.S. tribal casinos. For an overview of the U.S. experience, see Andrew Light and Kathryn Rand, *Indian Gaming and Tribal Sovereignty: The Casino Compromise* (Lawrence: University Press of Kansas, 2005).

5. For a detailed overview of the emergence of Indigenous gaming in Canada, see Yale Belanger, *Gambling with the Future: The Evolution of Aboriginal Gaming in Canada* (Saskatoon: Purich Publishing, 2006); and Yale Belanger, ed., *First Nations Gaming in Canada* (Winnipeg: University of Manitoba Press, 2011).
6. I detail the complex history of Casino Rama in Darrel Manitowabi, "From Fish Weirs to Casino: Negotiating Neoliberalism at Mnjikaning" (PhD diss., University of Toronto, 2007); and Darrel Manitowabi, "Casino Rama: First Nations Self-Determination, Neoliberal Solution, or Partial Middle-Ground?" in Belanger, *First Nations Gaming in Canada*, 255–78. In sum, provinces in Canada have jurisdiction over gaming, and similar to the U.S. experience, First Nations must enter an agreement with the province to pursue gaming. There is no federal act in Canada permitting Indigenous gaming.
7. See, for example, Light and Rand, *Indian Gaming and Tribal Sovereignty*; and Belanger, *First Nations Gaming in Canada*. For comparative ethnographic accounts, see Eve Darian-Smith, *New Capitalists: Law, Politics, and Identity Surrounding Casino Gaming on Native American Land* (Toronto: Nelson, 2004); and Jessica Cattelino, *High Stakes: Florida Seminole Gaming and Sovereignty* (Durham, NC: Duke University Press, 2008).
8. Some Indigenous North American peoples have deliberately chosen to exclude cultural self-representations at their casinos. For example, Cattalino remarks that for the Seminole in Florida, "casinos are their business, not their culture." Cattalino, *High Stakes*, 30.
9. Mary Lawlor, *Public Native America: Tribal Self-Representation in Museums, Powwows, and Casinos* (New Brunswick, NJ: Rutgers University Press, 2006). Lawlor also examines the Navajo Nation Museum and the Wind River Shoshone and Arapaho Cultural Center and Powwow and how they relate to Indigenous internationalism.
10. This is a contested issue in discussions about the Mashantucket Pequot, especially as it relates to motivations surrounding the regaining of tribal status and problematic discussions on "authenticity." See Lawlor, *Public Native America*, 31–41.
11. Ibid., 36–55. As part of my PhD fieldwork I visited both the Pequot museum and casino and made comparative observations.
12. Ibid., 133–53.
13. Ibid., 154.
14. Ibid., 5.
15. John J. Bodinger de Uriarte, *Casino and Museum: Representing Mashantucket Pequot*

Identity (Tucson: University of Arizona Press, 2007).

16. Up until regaining tribal status, the Pequot were assumed to no longer exist; see Lawlor, *Public Native America*, and Bondinger de Uriarte, *Casino and Museum*.

17. Bondinger de Uriarte, *Casino and Museum*, 69–76.

18. David Cuillier and Susan Dente Ross, "Gambling with Identity: Self-Representation of American Indians on Official Tribal Websites," *Howard Journal of Communications* 18 (2007): 197–219.

19. Ibid., 204, 206.

20. Ibid., 208.

21. Ibid., 211–12.

22. John Comoraff and Jean Comoraff, *Ethnicity, Inc.* (Chicago: University of Chicago Press, 2009).

23. Celeste C. Lacroix, "High Stakes Stereotypes: The Emergence of the 'Casino Indian' Trope in Television Depictions of Contemporary Native Americans," *Howard Journal of Communications* 22 (2011): 1–23.

24. "M'njikaning Art Studio," Library and Archives Canada, http://www.collectionscanada. gc.ca/eppp-archive/100/205/301/ic/cdc/simcoeregion/business/mnjikaning/m_studio. htm.

25. In a pamphlet produced by Casino Rama and the Mnjikaning Art Studio, the artists cite the teachings of Benton-Banai as found in his book Mishomis. See the back of the cover of the information pamphlet by the Mnjikaning Art Studio, *Welcome to the Mnjikaning Art Wall of Casino Rama* (Rama, ON: Mnjikaning Art Studio, n.d.); and Edward Benton-Banai, *The Mishomis Book: The Voice of the Ojibway* (Hayward, WI: Indian Country Communications, 1988).

26. In my descriptions of the clans, I am summarizing information directly from Mnjikaning Art Studio, *Welcome to the Mnjikaning Art Wall.*

27. Ibid.

28. Chief Yellowhead, or "Musquakie," was the ancestral chief of the community when the reserve was created in 1836. See Peter S. Schmalz, *The Ojibwa of Southern Ontario* (Toronto: University of Toronto Press, 1991), 128.

29. My description of the rotunda and hotel is based on information in "Casino Rama Hotel: Grand Opening. A Packet & Times Special Advertising Feature," *Packet and Times* (September 2002), 1–12; it is supplemented by my field notes and participant observation (2002–2004).

30. "Casino Rama Hotel," 9.

31. After some initial planning and consultation, it was determined not to be cost-effective

to build a museum or cultural center; thus the focus of the department centered on community cultural activities.

32. The activities of the department were at times political. For example, Mnjikaning made a financial contribution to the expansion of the nearby Orillia Soldier's Memorial Hospital. In recognition of this, the hospital considered space for traditional medicine and consulted with the Chippewas of Rama on this matter.

33. There are two formal Christian religions in the community, the United Church and the Presbyterian Church. As well, some community members practice Anishinaabe spirituality by regular sweats and attendance at ceremonies. Religion is diverse in the community.

34. Author's field notes.

35. "Anishinaabemowin" means the "Anishinaabe language."

36. Ibid.

37. For instance, for a study on the James Bay Cree equivalent, see Naomi Adelson, *"Being Alive Well": Health and the Politics of Cree Well-Being* (Toronto: University of Toronto Press, 2004). For a study on the Plains Cree equivalent, see Michael Hart, *Seeking Mino-Pimatisiwin: An Aboriginal Approach to Helping* (Halifax, NS: Fernwood, 2002).

38. For example, some studies use *bimaadiziwin* as a framework for Anishinaabe culture and well-being, but do not substantively situate it within the existing studies or make direct connections to the meaning of the term and its application. For a recent example, see Kevin Fitzmaurice, David Newhouse, and Tricia McGuire-Adams, *Well-Being in the Urban Aboriginal Community: Fostering Bimaadiziwin* (Toronto: Thompson, 2012). Here I summarize what I consider to be the literature that makes a substantive examination of the term as a reflection of Indigenous Anishinaabe culture and identity.

39. Depending on the dialect, "b" and "p" in *bimaadiziwin* are interchangeable, and there is no consistent spelling in either dialect.

40. A. Irving Hallowell, *Culture and Experience* (New York: Schocken, 1967), 360.

41. Ibid.

42. Midewiwin is the name of the Anishinaabe spiritual and healing society; see Benton-Banai, *Mishomis Book*.

43. James Dumont, *Culture, Behaviour, and Identity of the Native Person*, NATI 2105EZ University Course Manual (Sudbury, ON: University of Sudbury, 1989), 146–47.

44. Roger Spielmann, *"You're So Fat!": Exploring Ojibwe Discourse* (Toronto: University of Toronto Press, 2002), 159.

45. Ibid., 159–60.

46. Leanne Simpson and Edna Manitowabi, "Theorizing Resurgence from within Nishnabeg

Thought," in *Centering Anishinaabeg Studies: Understanding the World through Stories,* ed. Jill Doerfler, Niigannwewidam Sinclair, and Heidi Stark (East Lansing: Michigan State University Press, 2013), 279–93.

47. Ibid.
48. Spielmann, *"You're So Fat!,"* 160.
49. I eventually learned that tension existed between community members and non-Aboriginal people employed in upper management positions in the First Nation administration. See Manitowabi, *From Fish Weirs to Casino*; and Manitowabi, "Casino Rama."
50. Author's field notes 2002.
51. When I returned to the casino in 2011, the carpets were no longer there.
52. "M'njikaning Art Studio."
53. *Chippewas of Mnjikaning First Nation,* 22.
54. Maurice Merleau-Ponty, *The Primacy of Perception; and Other Essays,* ed. James Edie (Evanston, IL: Northwestern University Press, 1964), 161, 168.
55. Colin Scott, "Spirit and Practical Knowledge in the Person of the Bear among Wemindji Cree Hunters," *Ethnos* 71, no. 1 (2006): 51–66.
56. Tim Ingold, *The Perception of the Environment: Essays on Livelihood, Dwelling and Skill* (London: Routledge, 2000), 56; Tim Ingold, "Rethinking the Animate, Re-Animating Thought," *Ethnos* 71, no. 1 (2006): 11.
57. Frantz Fanon, *Black Skin, White Masks* (New York: Grove, 2008).

About the Contributors

Scott Andrews, a member of the Cherokee Nation of Oklahoma, is a professor in the English department and the American Indian Studies Program at California State University, Northridge. He has published reviews, essays, poetry, and fiction in various journals.

Yale D. Belanger is professor of political science at the University of Lethbridge. He is the author of *Gambling with the Future* (2006), and editor of *First Nations Gaming in Canada* (2011), and has published more than two dozen articles and book chapters about First Nations casinos and Aboriginal gambling.

Heid E. Erdrich is the author of five collections of poetry, including *National Monuments* and *Curator of Ephemera at the New Museum for Archaic Media*, which won the 2009 Minnesota Book Award. Erdrich's nonfiction work, *Original Local: Indigenous Foods, Stories and Recipes from the Upper Midwest*, was a City Pages 2014 Best Food Book.

Becca Gercken is an associate professor of English and American Indian studies at the University of Minnesota Morris. Her research interests include Plains ledger art, indigenous masculinities, and transindigenous literature. She is of Eastern Band Cherokee, Irish, and Pennsylvania Dutch descent.

LeAnne Howe, author of *Choctalking on Other Realities*, memoir, was the winner of the inaugural 2014 MLA Prize for Studies in Native American Literatures, Cultures, and Languages. Howe received the Western Literature Association's 2015 Distinguished Achievement Award for her body of literature. Born and raised in Oklahoma, Howe, an enrolled citizen of the Choctaw Nation of Oklahoma, has given readings of her work around the world, and her awards include the Fulbright Scholarship 2010–2011 to Jordan, the 2012 Lifetime Achievement Award from the Native Writers Circle of the Americas, and a 2012 United States Artists Ford Fellowship. She is the Eidson Distinguished Professor at the University of Georgia, Athens.

Darrel Manitowabi, a citizen of the Wiikwemkoong Unceded Territory, currently resides in the Whitefish River First Nation. He is associate professor in the School of Northern and Community Studies, Anthropology Program, at Laurentian University, Sudbury, Ontario. He has a PhD in sociocultural anthropology from the University of Toronto and has published articles on Indigenous gaming, Ojibwa/Anishinaabe ethnohistory, urban Indigenous issues, and Indigenous health.

Meghan Y. McCune is an assistant professor of anthropology and sociology and a director of social sciences at Jamestown Community College. She earned her PhD in anthropology from Michigan State University. Her academic interests include Indigenous sovereignty, specifically Haudenosaunee land rights and economic development; federal policy and Indian law; legal anthropology; whiteness; social class; intersectionality; and discourse analysis. She currently resides with her husband and daughter in Salamanca on the Seneca Nation of Indians' Allegany Territory.

Caroline Laurent has a master of power, discourse, writing from the University of Orléans, France and a master of tribal administration and governance from the University of Minnesota Duluth. She also holds a PhD in history from the Sorbonne University, Paris. Her dissertation is entitled "The Impact of Gaming on Minnesota Tribal Nations: The Case of the Mille Lacs Band of Ojibwe, 1976–2016."

Julie Pelletier is of Maliseet, Mi'kmaq, and French descent and from northern Maine. She teaches in the Indigenous studies department at the University of Winnipeg and earned her MA and PhD at Michigan State University's Department of Anthropology. Her research and action interests include indigenizing the academy, Indigenous identity, and Indigenous economic development strategies.